Conquering College

A Guide for Undergraduates

Victor L. Cahn

ROWMAN & LITTLEFIELD EDUCATION
Lanham • *New York* • *Toronto* • *Plymouth, UK*

Published in the United States of America
by Rowman & Littlefield Education
A Division of Rowman & Littlefield Publishers, Inc.
A wholly owned subsidiary of The Rowman & Littlefield Publishing Group, Inc.
4501 Forbes Boulevard, Suite 200, Lanham, Maryland 20706
www.rowmaneducation.com

Estover Road
Plymouth PL6 7PY
United Kingdom

British Library Cataloguing in Publication Information Available

Library of Congress Cataloging-in-Publication Data

Cahn, Victor L.
  Conquering college : a guide for undergraduates / Victor L. Cahn.
    p. cm.
  ISBN 978-1-60709-187-5 (cloth : alk. paper) — ISBN 978-1-60709-188-2
(pbk. : alk. paper) — ISBN 978-1-60709-189-9 (electronic)
  1. College student orientation—United States. I. Title.

  LB2343.32.C33 2009
  378.1'98—dc22   2009003904

∞™ The paper used in this publication meets the minimum requirements of
American National Standard for Information Sciences—Permanence of
Paper for Printed Library Materials, ANSI/NISO Z39.48-1992.
Manufactured in the United States of America.

To Steven,
my brother and my friend

Contents

1 You're Accepted 1

2 Why Are You Going? 5

3 Ready to Go 9
A New Start
Maintaining Perspective

4 An Overview of the Curriculum 15
Your Responsibility
Requirements
Your Major
Your General Education
Summing Up

5 The Faculty 33
An Overall View
Publish or Perish
Tenure
Academic Strata
Evaluating Teachers

6 Creating Your Program 43
Preliminary Thinking
Making Choices
Finding the Right Teachers

Finding the Right Courses
Constructing Your Schedule

7 Carrying Out Your Program   51
Attending Class
In Class
Outside Class

8 Working With the Faculty   67
Visiting
Concerning Papers
Complaints
Problems With Teachers
Letters of Recommendation

9 Beyond the Classroom   77
Living at College
Extracurricular Life
Alternative Credit

10 Final Words   95

About the Author   99

Chapter One

You're Accepted

Let's begin with a familiar scenario.

Last spring, you regularly reached into your mailbox, seeking an envelope from a college you had designated as one of your top choices. You hoped that the envelope would be thick, for then it would contain not only a letter of acceptance but also questionnaires about, among other matters, dormitory and roommate preference. A fatal thin envelope would hold only a single page that delicately explained why you, along with so many other qualified applicants, had been rejected.

Those of you who eventually cradled thick envelopes from the "right" schools reveled in your good fortune, confident that your futures were assured. Those stuck with thin envelopes from all but a few reputedly less desirable institutions drooped inconsolably, convinced that your dreams were doomed.

Both portraits are understandable, but both are based on misconceptions about college life.

The chief premise of this book is that the quality of your undergraduate education rests with you, the student. Whatever the claims by prominent guidebooks and magazines, no school guarantees a path to learning. All any school can offer is the chance to learn, and every one does so in essentially the same way.

Students everywhere study similar materials. No college has secret plays of Shakespeare hidden in its library stacks. The same table of elements hangs in chemistry labs across the country. Plato and Aristotle raise the same issues in Montana as they do in Massachusetts. Virtually every school requires you to read books, take exams, write papers, and complete reports.

Outside the classroom as well, most colleges are much alike. Virtually all have gymnasiums, and virtually all sponsor varsity teams and intramural sports. Virtually all offer musical and theatrical productions, and virtually all have a newspaper, yearbook, radio station, and literary magazine, in addition to scientific societies, political clubs, and religious and service organizations.

Every school has accomplished faculty ready to work with you, and every school has administrative and support staff prepared to help smooth your way.

The key is how you meet the opportunities and challenges inherent in these offerings.

A brilliant professor may be engaged with gifted students in a magnificent building on a picturesque campus. But if you haven't done the reading, or if you're not listening, or if you haven't bothered to show up, you're out of it. One opportunity is down the proverbial drain.

On the other hand, the professor may be uninspired, your fellow students distracted, the classroom bleak, and the campus gloomy. But if you're someone who reads, studies, and thinks, you'll graduate as an educated person.

I'll be fair, though. All schools are not interchangeable.

Some enjoy extraordinary reputations, and a degree from them carries undeniable prestige. To be sure, reputations may become sullied. Nevertheless, certain colleges have enjoyed places of honor for a long time, and will likely do so for just as long a time to come.

Different schools also have different emphases. Some stress the sciences, and boast research facilities that are astonishingly rich. Others specialize in the performing arts, and provide exceptional music, theater, and dance programs.

The size of an institution matters, too.

At a liberal arts college, with an enrollment of 2500 or so, the student population is comprised entirely of freshmen, sophomores, juniors, and seniors. Classes tend to be small, so that personal attention is not only available, but expected. Yet the intimacy of the environment ensures that certain curricular and extracurricular opportunities will be limited, and that the same faces will reappear inside classrooms and along walkways.

At a university, on the other hand, many thousands of undergraduates share the campus with many thousands of graduate students enrolled in medical or law school, business or engineering school, or any of several dozen doctoral programs. Thus some people inevitably feel lost amid a labyrinthine campus and classes that seem more like rallies. Still, the wealth of academic and extracurricular possibilities, as well as the magnitude and intensity of the surrounding action, exhilarates countless others.

Some schools offer the pastoral calm of a rural setting, others the bustle of urban life. Some colleges remain single-sex, although for males this alternative has about vanished. Some schools have a religious or military affiliation.

Don't, however, overestimate these variations. *What students find at college matters far less than what they bring to it.*

$$\approx\hspace{-0.5em}\mathcal{O}$$

At this juncture, I'll assume that you have completed your application and acceptance procedures, and begun to prepare for departure to the campus.

Now you are ready to muse on the most important distinction between high school and college: freedom. As an undergraduate, you'll be granted all sorts of independence: academic, social, and personal. You may be accustomed to parents and teachers hovering about, telling you what to do, and trying to impose their rules on your life. At college you devise your own rules. You run your life.

In the academic domain, you select your program. You establish your daily schedule and decide how closely you follow it. You decide when, where, and how you study. You decide how to move through the day to fulfill responsibilities.

With regard to personal matters, you decide when, where, and what you eat. You decide when to sleep and shower. You decide when and if to clean your room and launder your clothes. Eventually you decide on your living quarters and roommates.

In the social sphere, you decide whether to go out at night. You decide whether to attend a certain party or join a particular group of companions. You decide how to conduct yourself on these excursions. You decide when to return.

One reason so many students who triumph in high school subsequently flounder in college is that they have yet to learn to think and act for themselves. They function only when others dictate, and when at college no one tells them what to do, they do nothing. Or the wrong thing. In contrast are those students who feel thwarted by high-school restrictions, but who in college blossom under their newly found autonomy.

You're on your own, just as in life. And no matter who you are or what you've done thus far, you won't know if you can meet this challenge until you try.

Chapter Two

Why Are You Going?

For some readers, the answer to this question is obvious: "I want a good job, and I need a college degree to get one." On the other hand, perhaps you find yourself attending only because friends are, or because everyone you know assumes that you'll comply with expectations.

Any of these responses is reasonable, but I think yours ought to be more sophisticated. In fact, to benefit most from college, you ought to know precisely why you're there, so you'll be better prepared to make appropriate choices.

First, contrast your high-school curriculum with the one offered at a typical college. How many secondary school students have taken courses in philosophy, psychology, geology, economics, anthropology, linguistics, sociology, or political science? How many even know what these subjects are about? How many of the brightest and most talented have explored select areas of history, literature, art, and music? Or biology, chemistry, physics, and mathematics? How many have become fluent in reading, writing, and speaking a second or third language?

Here's the heart of what college presents: the opportunity to encounter new fields and delve further into others.

Perhaps you're confident that you don't need to explore. You know what you like, and you know what career you want. Quite a few incoming college students feel precisely that way.

Yet no matter how positive you are, you might, like millions of other people, change your mind, for what appeals to you at eighteen may be of no interest when you're twenty-one. At twenty-five you might find

5

your priorities altered once more, and again at thirty-five, and even at forty.

Let me dramatize this notion with a personal example. After reading whatever biographical information about me is included in this book, you may be surprised to learn that I started college as a premed. During my first chemistry course, roughly a day and a half in, I began to have doubts, and in my own mind I shifted to music, all the while contemplating history.

Eventually I became an English major, but I still wasn't sure what profession would suit me best. I investigated journalism, television, publishing, and advertising.

I never considered teaching.

I ended up teaching.

My point is that after college, all these alternatives were available. You may enter certain that you're going to work in sales. You may leave with the same ambition. Fine. But after four years of intellectual and social adventure, you may depart with an entirely different vision of yourself, because college can have that powerful an impact.

Now let's put aside matters of occupation. Whether you hope to be an engineer, a journalist, a chef, or a construction worker, whether a college diploma is essential for your job, a college education is something you want.

These four years are the only period of your life when you are encouraged to probe the entire range of human thought and endeavor. They are the only ones when your primary responsibility is to read, study, think, and question.

In high school you're busy following one bell after another. Classes meet every day, you're assigned most of your courses and teachers, and you conform to a standard curriculum with little chance to pursue your own interests.

When you leave college, you begin to specialize. If you attend medical or law school, your existence is dominated by work in that one field. The same is true if you go to graduate school. If you plunge into the workplace, you spend eight or nine hours at your employment. None of these alternatives leaves much room for general study.

Only in college do you have time and freedom to explore.

Here's one reason I feel sorry for those students who dash through college in three years. In cases of financial exigency I understand, but I've never found such necessity to be the reason. No, three-year graduates are always hurrying to fill the position that will absorb them for the next forty-five years. And whenever I meet those students down the road, they always regret that they curtailed their undergraduate experience.

Can you educate yourself outside school? Possibly. If you're strongly disciplined, you can read philosophy and history on your own. But mastering difficult subject matter is easier with teachers and fellow students working in a structured environment where the material is organized and presented to help you learn. At college, education is, or ought to be, your prime pursuit. The entire curriculum is yours. The library, the labs, and all the rest of the facilities are yours. They never will be again.

Some of you are convinced that you're not interested in the entire curriculum. You don't care about linguistics or sociology, art or psychology. You want to prepare for a job, find that job, and proceed with your life.

Then may I ask one more question? Are you at all interested in people, events, and the world around you? I hope the answer is "yes." If it isn't, you can stop reading now.

But if you do possess such concerns, then college is the place to develop your mind and, I daresay, your heart. You started in elementary school, but college is where you can progress with the greatest vigor.

Why? Because in college you read and study as much as you want. Classes meet as seldom as once a week. You set your schedule. To a great extent you choose your courses, and you choose completely your extracurricular program. Never again, may I remind you, will you have such freedom.

Therefore, at this stage, don't worry about your job. What you learn at college will help you in whatever direction you go. Most important, what you learn at college will help you as a citizen and as a thinking, feeling human being.

Here's the central reason you're going to college: not to prepare for a career, although that part may work out, but *to prepare for life.*

This preparation will take many forms.

You may be accustomed to dispensing opinions and having listeners in and out of school applaud. At college, however, teachers and students will challenge your political, ethical, aesthetic, and religious values. At times your fundamental convictions may be shaken. You may retain them. You may acquire new ones.

In the classroom and dormitory, and across the campus, you will encounter people who bring you new perspectives. Indeed, their influence may be more lasting than the strictly academic. A classmate from another country, a roommate from another background: these individuals may change you profoundly.

In this book, our focus will be one aspect of the extravaganza: planning and carrying out your academic program, a task that falls into my field of expertise (he says modestly). I've been teaching for thirty-five years, with nearly thirty of those at the college level. I've also talked to thousands of students and observed countless more, and I like to think I've learned something. In addition, I was, as you know, a student myself, and, as you will learn, not always a successful one. Perhaps reading about my missteps will encourage you. Besides, I may be old (check that: I *am* old), but I remember my struggles, so I sympathize with yours.

Despite my emphasis, however, academics are not the totality of the undergraduate environment. Therefore we'll also consider the whirligig of activity outside the classroom.

Whatever the immediate subject, though, this book will proceed according to one principle: *the purpose of a college education is to prepare you for life.*

Chapter Three

Ready to Go

A NEW START

College represents a fresh start. This assertion may seem obvious, but it's worth stating.

You'll soon discover, if you're not aware already, that we carry the experiences of junior high and high school for a long time. Our victories and, especially, our failures weigh heavily, partly because when we are young, we undergo constant change, all the while questioning who we are and how we see ourselves. Therefore we are so vulnerable to the judgments of others that trivial events may acquire terrifying import.

You know what I mean. The missed shot in the big game; the date that never took place, or the one that did but was so depressing; the botched oral report: these assume an enormity that allows them to haunt us forever. Even when we recognize their ultimate insignificance, we retain the painful memories. For the rest of your life, you may think of yourself competing against high-school rivals, desperately trying to prove that you deserve the respect they never granted you.

Leave aside such baggage. Contemplate instead that no one at college remembers what happened to you in high school. The ball you dropped? The election you lost? Nobody cares.

Few will be interested in your triumphs, either. Let's say you were the star of your class: president, valedictorian, editor of the newspaper, captain of three teams. Congratulations, but you can't live on those glories any longer.

It's a new ballgame, everybody.

MAINTAINING PERSPECTIVE

I'll offer one more general reflection about college life, with emphasis on the opening days.

Let's assume that you've arrived for the beginning of the school year. You've located the administration building, and someone there has given you a key and directions to your dormitory. You've found your room, you've unpacked, and your family has departed.

Now you size up your situation: for perhaps the first time, you're genuinely on your own.

You've been smart enough to read the college catalogue from cover to cover. You're familiar with school regulations, you've gained a sense of the courses and programs, and you have some feel for the layout of the campus.

Now let's move ahead seventy-two hours, when matters have become more chaotic. You've rambled through an elaborate orientation schedule, packed with lectures, discussions, activities, tours, dinners, movies, more lectures, and parties. You've accrued useful information, but you've also found the procedure exhausting. Moreover, meeting so many people has left you nonplussed, especially after the first students-only reception, where campus leaders and their cohorts introduced you to some of the rowdier aspects of college life.

Meanwhile you've been shuffled through a maze of lines and offices. You've signed your name on a dozen forms, you've had your picture taken (and your eyes were closed, you think), you've opened charge accounts, you've signed more forms, you've shaken the hands of smiling administrators, you've been lost in buildings and along pathways, and you've signed your name a dozen more times. You've been given a schedule of classes and told that some professor somewhere is your faculty advisor.

In brief, only three days into your college career, and you're dizzy.

Here is the time to remember one rule for survival and success at college, not only during the first weeks, but throughout the four years: if you have a problem, talk to somebody.

Begin with your colleagues. Many colleges designate certain seniors and juniors as house residents or floor counselors. These paid volunteers live in the dormitory and have the advantage of being close to your age. They might also have undergone some of the same difficulties you're encountering, and in the same environment. Remember, though, that residents are themselves students and may lack seasoning. They may also have troubles of their own that will skew their judgment. Still, a good floor counselor should not be overlooked.

Don't overlook members of the faculty, either. If you have an advisor, find that person and ask every question on your mind. The odds are that you'll receive intelligent responses to at least a few dilemmas, but even if the advisor proves to be less than a gold mine of information, the visit will probably lead you in a constructive direction. Besides, the very act of talking will make you feel better.

If your advisor can't be found, try another faculty office. You may be snubbed, as ruder souls complain that they have issues of their own, and, hey, can't you find your advisor? If so, smile and walk on. More likely, though, whatever office you enter, the occupant will be amiable. That's one pleasing quality about a campus. Faculty and staff are accustomed to solving quandaries, and many of us genuinely enjoy working with students.

If no helpful professors are around, turn to a member of the administration. Don't bother the provost or the dean of faculty. Both have enough to worry about and, strictly speaking, you're not their responsibility. Instead, find the office of the dean of students, the dean of the college, or the local version thereof. Then start talking. Administrators deal regularly with parents and other representatives of the outside world and thus have a down-to-earth viewpoint. They are also expert at maneuvering around seemingly impassable regulations. Sometimes when you break college rules, administrators must confront you, your family, or even the law. But when you mean well, they can be of enormous help.

One note of caution: be prepared to encounter bureaucracy. All large organizations thrive on red tape, and colleges are no different. Whatever happens, keep cool.

After you've talked with an official, you'll realize that most of your problems are less daunting than you imagined. The notable exception will be the matter of courses, and you are currently holding a book to help in this area.

In short, don't be timid. Whatever the annoyance, don't let it fester. Talk to somebody.

Talk to departmental assistants or secretaries. They deal constantly with the panorama of characters that populate a college and thereby acquire patience and understanding. Their competence keeps schools functioning, and their warmth and wisdom soothe befuddled souls of every rank.

I'll mention one cause for the need to talk that occurs more often than students acknowledge. During the first night or two, perhaps longer, you may be homesick. One of the ironies of the opening days is that as you feel lonely, your misery is compounded by the apparent confidence everyone else exudes. Some students may admit that they'd prefer to be at the movies, or with friends, or at the beach, but rarely will people openly confess that they miss their families.

What's your recourse? A few phone calls or an exchange of e-mails is usually helpful, but if those aren't sufficient, talk to somebody. Try your fellow students, try faculty, try members of the administration, try secretaries, try the custodial crew. But talk to somebody. And if problems become overpowering, visit the professional counseling staff that every school maintains to help you navigate rough times. Feel no embarrassment about stopping by this office. We all need advice; you're just smart enough ask for it.

One other deception you might pull on yourself. As you wander across the campus, you will be convinced that the rest of the community is striding with purpose, that they all know just where they're going and what to do when they get there, that you're the only pathetic soul in sight.

Don't let them fool you. During the first week, everybody's buffaloed, from freshmen to veteran faculty. Students are shifting in and out of classes, standing in one endless line to purchase books, then in another to sell those books, then returning to the first one to buy a new supply. Meanwhile they're worried about their course load, their roommate, their speeding ticket from last night, their date for tonight, their dining room account, everything. Professors are also scrambling as they complete syllabi and other opening-day handouts, all the while signing student schedules and nervously anticipating new classes. Half the time at least one textbook order comes in wrong, so faculty, too, must shove through the bookstore mobs.

In a couple of weeks, all will be calm. Once classes are in progress, you'll fall into a rhythm as familiar as the one you left a few months ago.

Just keep in mind one rule: *talk to somebody.*

Chapter Four

An Overview of the Curriculum

YOUR RESPONSIBILITY

We have now arrived at the main section of this book. Handling courses will almost certainly be the cornerstone of your college career.

What may unnerve you initially is the numbers of choices, since, as we noted earlier, in high school such options were limited. You were probably allowed to select which foreign language to study and whether to continue it at upper levels. You may have been permitted to decide whether to take higher mathematics, chemistry, physics, art, and music. Finally, you were probably asked to choose between regular or honors sections.

Otherwise, I assume, you were handed a program. You were almost certainly required to take four years of English, as well as semesters of history, science, and mathematics, and you might well have been required to take a foreign language. You were probably assigned to teachers, and given very little choice about class hours.

At college, all of this changes. You are expected to examine a master schedule and create a program for yourself, concurrently ensuring that you're fulfilling requirements for graduation as well as those for your major. When you complete your formulation, you will probably show it to your advisor, who is supposed to affirm that it is both legal and logical.

Here is the place to note another difference between secondary school and college. Imagine that during the spring semester of your senior year you were informed that you had failed to accumulate sufficient credits for graduation or that you had neglected to complete a required course. As a result, you would not be able to graduate. How would you react?

With outrage, I presume. The school assigned your courses. Any mistakes were theirs, not yours, and you shouldn't suffer the consequences.

But if that sort of calamity arises at college, you'll have no one to blame but yourself. Don't expect your advisor to shoulder responsibility for your program. Even if both of you inspect your course selection carefully, but still miscalculate your credits, the culpability will lie with you.

In college, you have freedom to choose. Yet as I have said before, and doubtless will repeat, freedom demands responsibility. You are responsible for your program.

By the way, after you received your original letter of acceptance and submitted the deposit confirming that you would attend this school, you likely received another series of forms, one of which asked you to compose a schedule for the upcoming semester. You did your best to select wisely, but, as will soon become apparent, a program can be created properly only when you are on campus, or at least more familiar with courses and personnel. In any case, when you arrive, you may be handed a schedule based on this blind summer determination. The scheme was likely designed by a computer, with help from members of the Academic Affairs Office, but no matter how it was concocted, it is not binding. You can change anything you want. Whether you care to do so is another matter, but you're allowed, and during the first week, or as long as the school permits, you can add and drop classes.

College courses can be divided into three general categories. I'll describe them briefly, then proceed in detail through each.

The first group includes those required for the bachelor's degree. Some schools demand many such requirements, others none. Be sure you understand your college's system.

The second set includes those courses needed for your major. Virtually every school demands that you select one subject in which you will concentrate, and every department has its own regulations. For instance, if you focus on history, you will have to take a certain number of classes within the department, including a couple intended especially for majors. You might pursue instead a preprofessional major, such as premed or prelaw. Some students double major, fulfilling requirements for two departments. Other students follow a self-determined major, devising their own specialization that involves offerings from several fields

The final category of courses includes electives, courses that you take of your own volition. Some will be in areas of peripheral interest. Some will meet at a convenient time or otherwise seem to be an obliging way to complete your program.

REQUIREMENTS

When I graduated from Columbia College in 1969, degree requirements were stringent, and I spent most of my freshman and sophomore years fulfilling them. For instance, for the past eighty years or so, all Columbia students have taken a two-year sequence called "Contemporary Civilization" ("CC" for short). The first year includes a history of Western thought based on common texts used by dozens of sections across the college. The second year's structure, which has altered over the decades, involves offerings from several departments. I chose two in anthropology.

I was also required to take a two-year sequence still called "Humanities." The first year encompasses a portion of what are sometimes referred to as "the Great Books." The fall semester is devoted to classical literature, primarily the Greek epic poems and tragic plays, and the spring term includes works from the past millennium, including Dante's *Inferno* and Swift's *Gulliver's Travels*. The second year is comprised of two single-term courses: one devoted to masterpieces of art, the other to those of music.

In my day, Columbia additionally demanded two years of laboratory science, mastery of a foreign language at the third-year level, and a year of English composition. For good measure, we had to pass four semesters of physical education, including a swimming test.

All these impositions may sound cumbersome. Yet most schools have some version of them. CC and Humanities were and are unique to Columbia, but many institutions still demand something like a year of literature or composition, a year of laboratory science or math, or both, a couple of years of foreign language, and perhaps a class or two in philosophy, art, music, or history. In other words, a full range of what we call "liberal arts" courses.

"Unfair and unnecessary," you say. "I'm an adult. I can vote, drive, and go to war. Are you going to tell me that I'm not capable of choosing my classes? You must be kidding!"

To understand why we're not, glance at a college diploma. You'll notice that it says something to the effect of "the faculty awards" the degree. This line is crucial. The diploma is in essence a statement by the faculty that the recipient has completed a program that constitutes an education. Well, if all we ask is that you take a certain number of classes, then that's all the diploma means. Whether they amount to what the faculty judges to be a real education is not at all certain. Requirements, however, guarantee that you complete courses which in sum assure us that you have acquired the breadth and depth of knowledge that we, the faculty, believe a graduate of our institution should achieve. Thus when we award the diploma, we stand behind it.

I know this explanation makes us sound a mite arrogant, but you're going to carry that diploma for the rest of your life as proof of the quality of your education. If you expect the faculty to endorse your degree, and you certainly expect future employers to respect it, then the faculty ought to have the salient voice in determining what we are endorsing. Setting standards in the form of requirements is an expression of that voice.

"But if I have to take a course, I won't like it. And if I don't like it, I won't work hard, I won't learn, and the whole thing will be a waste." So goes a familiar lament.

Calm down. If the course proves worthwhile, you'll soon forget that it was required. So will everybody else in the class. I assure you that your liking or disliking a course will have little to do with whether it is required.

In fact, you can assure yourself. Almost all your courses in high school were required. Didn't you like some of them? Ask yourself why they succeeded, then apply the same principle to college.

If you need a further reason for requirements, I have one. When you choose courses, the temptation is to stick with subjects you know, but this method is precisely the wrong way to proceed. Years ago, an English major advisee of mine announced that she wanted to branch out into the fine arts, which include painting, sculpture, and music. Pleased with her curiosity, I asked which courses she was considering. "Art history. That's what I like." Then I asked which era. "Impressionism," she said, "because I took it in high school, and really like it."

Would you agree that this young woman was not demonstrating the proper spirit?

These days most colleges help you explore. They don't necessarily demand that you take specific courses, but rather that you fulfill "distribution credits." In other words, you must select a couple of classes from each of the three major divisions of the curriculum: the humanities, which include art, music, literature, and philosophy; the social sciences, which include history, government, and economics; and the natural sciences, which include biology, chemistry, and physics.

Every school proceeds differently in this area, and no general description encompasses all. Indeed, some institutions refuse to impose any requirements, and you might have been attracted to such places precisely because they guarantee such license.

They're not doing you a favor. When you open a college catalogue, you come across entire departments about which you know nothing. Here, as we said earlier, is one reason to attend college. Once you begin fulfilling requirements, though, you'll learn what these departments offer, and such knowledge can only help in what we have established as your overarching goal at college: to prepare for life. You might confirm that a subject you anticipated disliking is in fact not for you. You are more likely to learn that a new subject is fascinating, and such discoveries change people's visions of themselves and their futures. Almost all college graduates remember at least one course that proved a revelation. They may have entered the class knowing little, but at the end of the term they saw their worlds differently. That's what college can do for you. And requirements help.

In the middle of your college years, the time will come when you will choose a major. Yet from your first day on campus you will be badgered about whether you've made this choice. If you confess you haven't, you'll be told to start thinking, and fast. Deans, advisors, counselors, teachers, and your own colleagues will urge you to finalize plans for specialization.

Pay no attention to these people. They mean well, most of them, but they're missing the point.

A cardinal reason you're in college is to investigate unfamiliar areas of inquiry. I was lucky, because Columbia forced me. You, however, may not have it so easy. If your school doesn't have requirements that push you, you have to push yourself to take curricular risks. Sticking with the familiar is often agreeable. Yet those risks may prove more valuable.

A last thought about requirements. You may be tempted to leave them until your third or fourth year, rationalizing, "College is so hard at the beginning. I'll just take what I like." Meanwhile you hope that farther down the road, requirements will magically disappear.

Exactly the opposite happens. The longer you put them off, the more intrusive they become. Take these courses early, when you haven't chosen your field of concentration, and you have room on your program. But don't take them just to "get rid of them." Understand that you're taking requirements because they open your eyes to the entire curriculum. Then when you finally do select a major, you'll decide on the basis of wide experience, not on the same few subjects you knew after high school.

YOUR MAJOR

The second consideration in choosing courses is your major field, which you formally declare somewhere in the middle of your college career. Yet a good many students delay the decision, some until their senior years. The only problem with choosing late is that during your final semesters you may have to squeeze in certain classes needed to fulfill departmental demands. But since these will be in your favorite subject, you won't mind. Otherwise an early affirmation is rarely an advantage.

Many first-year students have some idea of their major. Remember, though, that quite a few people enter with specific ambitions but soon view matters differently. For instance, you may stroll into your first college math class thinking yourself a hotshot mathematician. After all, you earned one of the top grades in your high-school calculus class. But within a few weeks, as you work among other big guns, you may discover that you are of lesser caliber. At times, reality rears its ugly head, and although disillusionment may be hard to accept, better to learn your limitations now.

I know that some students begin college certain of their major, and from the first day they never falter. If you are one of these folks, my hat's off to you, as long as the selection is your own, and you're happy.

But for very few does the question resolve itself so neatly, so to the legion of those "undecided" I offer the following admonitions.

The primary consideration in determining your major is to pick a subject you enjoy, one that stimulates or, we hope, fascinates you. Don't make yourself suffer to impress anyone else, including those who tell you that a certain major looks good on a résumé. Choose a subject you genuinely like.

Two, talk to older students majoring in your prospective department. If they're pleased, good. If they're disappointed, ask why, and consider whether what bothers them will annoy you.

Three, check that you can live under the regulations the individual department imposes. Every one establishes its own rules, so make sure you are comfortable with those you will have to follow. If the department requires an inordinate number of courses, or a few that you know you will find unpleasant, be careful. If you do not like several of the department's professors, be very careful. The department might insist that all majors write a thesis. If you doubt your ability or desire to complete so massive a tome, think hard about majoring there. Another subject will serve just as well.

Four, talk to a couple of professors about careers for which this field prepares you. See if the department has a record of what majors from the last five years have done. How many have gone to graduate school? How many have chosen jobs that might interest you?

Finally, keep in mind that the ideal major does not exist. Your foremost consideration is to make yourself content.

At the same time, don't neglect the rest of your education for this one field. If the major requires ten courses, take only ten. Ten is plenty. Ten is probably more than plenty. After all, this subject is only your major. It's not your life's work, at least not yet.

Here's a danger of the double major. If a single major demands ten courses, two majors will likely demand twenty. Now consider that your entire college experience may involve only thirty-two or thirty-six courses. If more than half are already determined, and if you add collegewide requirements that everyone has to take regardless of major, time quickly runs out.

Thus your major is important, but keep in mind our fundamental principle: you go to college not to prepare for a career, but to prepare for life.

YOUR GENERAL EDUCATION

Collegewide requirements eliminate some course options. Departmental requirements eliminate others. Yet you still have quite a few left, and these electives represent your best chance to exercise curricular freedom.

What follows is offered irrespective of a specific major or any college's requirements. If some suggestions fall under either category, you'll be left with more choice.

The Humanities

This division has lately been under attack from certain quarters. Many people, particularly those outside academia, question whether such subjects are "relevant." Do students of the humanities gain skills or knowledge that will contribute to success in "real life"?

In a word, yes.

Let's begin with literature, which is my field, so you may believe I'm biased. You're probably right. Even so, I think you'd agree that the abilities to read and write intelligently are useful in whatever career you follow. I am also convinced that such work sharpens your mind by demanding that you reason and imagine, and thereby develop both an active and a reflective intelligence.

What you read matters less to me than that you simply read, for almost anything you cover in college literature courses will help. If pressed, however, I make two recommendations.

The first is Shakespeare (admittedly one of my specialties, but, even so, go with me). Here is the writer acknowledged as the greatest the human race has produced, and he is no doubt the most influential. Furthermore, his plays are enthralling. Some of you surely dispute this claim, for you may have already read a couple and found the complex language a chore. Sometimes I'm sorry that Shakespeare is foisted on students unprepared to appreciate him.

Don't let such experiences discourage you. Four hundred years of audiences haven't singled out Shakespeare by chance, and his dramatizations of our emotions and intellects remain as rich as ever. If you want to understand how ambition and guilt can wreak havoc on the human character, read *Macbeth*. If you want to understand political power and its consequences, read the great tetralogy *Richard II*; *Henry IV, Part 1* and *Part 2*; and *Henry V*. If you want to understand the destructive nature of bigotry, read *The Merchant of Venice*. If you want to feel the redemptive power of love, try *King Lear*.

Are these plays difficult? Certainly. Few profound works are easily assimilated. But Western culture has embraced Shakespeare's oeuvre, and appreciating why is worth your time. Reading them may also change your perspective on life.

My other suggestion in the realm of literature is works of the classical era. I know that the subject sounds dull. All those Greeks and Romans talking about . . . well, you may not be sure what they're talking about. But I'll bet you've already enjoyed mythology, the basis of much of this material. Of all my students who have studied classical literature, such as Homer's *Iliad* and *Odyssey*, Virgil's *Aeneid*, and the great tragedies of Aeschylus, Sophocles, and Euripides, I cannot recall one who came away disappointed. These works are the foundation of Western culture. Nothing written over the past three thousand years matches them, except the plays of Shakespeare, and he's already part of your grand design.

If you read these masterpieces and nothing else, you're okay. I still urge you to read all you can, but these works are indispensable. I'm also confident that once you start with them, your curiosity will be piqued, and you'll want to read more.

While we're considering literature, I'll remind you to include a course in composition. I'm not talking about creative writing courses, where you write fiction or poetry. These can be wonderful, but I'm speaking of something else. I'm also not talking about certain forms of "freshman seminars," in which you study a narrow topic of interest to the teacher, and in which you write one or two papers. In such classes, reading and discussion take precedence over writing.

I'm advocating courses in which the priority is writing. You'll also read in these sections, perhaps nonfiction, fiction, poetry, or drama, but you'll focus at least as much on the qualities of good essays. Most important, you'll regularly put words on the page. The task is never easy, but it's far less daunting if you become accustomed to it. Don't run away from a course like composition because you're worried that it will be hard. College is the place to conquer your misgivings. If you don't do so here, you never will.

In this age, many people think that computer literacy has preempted traditional forms of communication. Not at all. The ability to write a crisp, coherent statement remains invaluable both in and out of school. Think of all the reports, papers, memos, and letters that are endemic to any profession. The more practice you have, the more facility you will acquire. In addition, the habit of writing, then reviewing, then correcting your own work, then rewriting, then rereading, and recorrecting until you're satisfied, will make you a sharper, more disciplined thinker.

Next I'll mention foreign language. I know that certain students find this subject tortuous, and a few seem to have a true language block. But for most people learning another language is possible. Furthermore, it is often useful, and in some careers vital. Nevertheless, studying a language is difficult. Classes at the introductory level meet several days a week, and the constant drill is arduous. In addition, you can't bluff your way through verb forms, idioms, and vocabulary. Either you know them or you don't, and the only way to learn them is to study. Such demands make students leery.

The benefits of knowing a second language are myriad. One, mastering a foreign language will give you a better grasp of the grammar and syntax of your own. Two, learning another language is the best way to understand the culture from which it emerges, an indispensable tool in this shrinking world. And three, whatever your field, the ability to write, read, and speak a second language is most impressive to prospective employers. When you have the capacity to go to Russia, Latin America, or the Far East and conduct business, you're special.

Next I'd recommend a course in classical music.

Yes, I hear the groans. I'm also aware that the vast majority of my readers have grown up listening to rock, hip-hop, heavy metal, or any of several dozen other categories. Even so, all of you know deep down, way deep down, that much popular music swiftly fades. You'll also acknowledge that certain other music will be played as long as civilization exists. Classical music, and by "classical" I mean works of Bach, Mozart, Beethoven, Brahms, Debussy, Wagner, and Stravinsky, among innumerable others, has survived a long time. Aren't you intrigued why it has aroused such fervor?

I'm confident that once you hear the music, you'll find it as enriching as the rest of the world does. I can't offer personal testimony about acquiring such appreciation, because I'm a violinist, and classical music has always been a part of my life. But at Columbia, that Humanities course in music I mentioned earlier probably changed more students than did any other offering in the curriculum. In fact, many who dragged themselves in on the first day departed at the end of the semester with the basis of a lifelong devotion.

Take a history of music or a course in the symphony or the Romantic Age. A good deal of class time will be spent listening, and most outside assignments will involve more listening. Such tasks are hardly displeasing. They also allow you to immerse yourself in something new that may alter your outlook on life.

I'd also recommend a course in the history of art, for that study will sharpen your vision of the environment. In addition, understanding artistic movements will help you understand the nature and path of our culture. So will learning what Rembrandt, Van Gogh, Brueghel, Renoir, and Picasso achieved, and why they matter to millions of people.

You will likely enjoy studying paintings, buildings, and sculpture. In addition, your own view of the world may be transformed.

An interjection.

One reason to experience literature, music, and art is that the study can be pleasurable. Remember, though, that the output of creative artists also reflects their eras and societies. Individual works may be appreciated independent of a specific environment, but all artists belong to their times and places. To understand the art is to understand the people, and to understand the people is to become educated.

Another result of studying literature, music, painting, architecture, and sculpture is the gradual realization that these fields reflect one another. Techniques, movements, and themes intersect, and when you make connections for yourself, the satisfactions are gratifying.

Back to our subject. I also urge you to take an introductory course in philosophy, probably in one of two varieties. The first is a history of ideas, beginning with the Greeks and continuing to Descartes, Hobbes, Hume, Kant, and perhaps some from our age. The other standard approach is a "problems" course, in which longstanding philosophical issues are discussed in the context of historical and contemporary thinkers.

Either class will inform you as to how influential ideas have developed, as well as provide insight into questions that have long puzzled humankind. Another benefit will be improving your acuity of thought.

You may have noticed that in proposing subjects throughout the humanities, I have listed mostly survey courses. Such a strategy is not accidental. I recall a friend who during his freshman year practically salivated in anticipation of a seminar devoted to Shakespeare's *King Lear*, arguably the greatest play ever written. What happened? In a few weeks, my friend was bored, and by the end of the semester he never wanted to hear about *King Lear* or Shakespeare again. Too often such courses serve the professor's interest, not yours. Let me emphasize that in college, especially in the first two years, you should strive for breadth. *Rather than learn a lot about a little, try to learn something about as much as possible.* Survey courses allow you a taste of everything. After you come across a particular artist, movement, or period that proves intriguing, you can specialize, perhaps with an eye on your career.

I'll repeat myself once more: you have only these four years to explore.

One other reason to take survey courses. If you were to ask professors what they judge to be the greatest deficiency in their students' academic background, the answer would be historical perspective. Stories abound about young people who confidently place events of the Renaissance during the Middle Ages, or for whom Chaucer was a writer of the eighteenth century, or according to whom Louis XIV was a leader of the Holy Roman Empire. Otherwise bright students can make astonishing misstatements about when Darwin lived, or when the Great Depression took place. One benefit of survey courses is that they almost always place material in a historical context.

And speaking of history . . .

The Social Sciences

As a whole, the social sciences are demanding. They require a good deal of specific information, and students sometimes shy away from courses in which facts and dates are inherent.

Your first priority in this division should be automatic: a course in American history, preferably a full-year study of the republic. Every school offers one, and you ought to take it. The vast majority of you are American citizens. Here is the country where you live, vote, and otherwise participate in the governmental process. To know the story of the country, the figures and events that have brought it to its present condition, is to prepare to help govern it.

I also recommend courses in European history. The compass of this field is extensive, given the numerous centuries and countries involved, but studying any aspect is valuable. My specific suggestions include the classical era (ancient Greece and Rome), and the Renaissance and Reformation, which mark the beginning of the modern world. Study, too, the French Revolution, as well as the social and intellectual upheavals of the nineteenth century. I hope you learn about the origins and consequences of the world wars. All such work will help you grapple with issues of our own time.

In your study of history, don't limit yourself to Western society. You are doubtless aware of the vital role that Eastern cultures play in the world, and a course in Middle Eastern history, or one about India, China, or Japan, is particularly valuable, given how much we deal with these areas and how little most of us know of them. Daily events permit tidbits of American and European history to permeate our minds. To many of us, however, the Eastern world remains largely a mystery, and college is the place to start unraveling it.

Consider a history course in a Third World country, or one about Africa or Latin America. From following the news, you realize how involved we are in these societies, and the more insight you have into them, the better equipped you are to analyze our actions and attitudes.

I know you can't take everything. All I urge is that you take as much history as possible.

Some of you may not agree with my thinking here. What possible relationship can events from hundreds of years ago have to those of today?

Think for a moment about the United States. The fundamentals of our current political debates originated during the military, judicial, and legislative struggles that formed the beginning of the republic. Those issues are also the ones we recall when we debate the direction of American policy. The Civil War took place in the middle of the nineteenth century, and the great wave of immigration began soon after, but many of the resulting divisions in our nation remain intrinsic to our lives. At the turn of the twentieth century, response to newly formed monopolies led to governmental action that still influences the business world you may enter. The New Deal legislation of the 1930s set the tone for social change that as yet affects you.

If you don't understand our country's past, you cannot look intelligently toward its future.

The same is true with the rest of the globe. I'll offer but one example. Conflict in the Middle East did not spring up over the last few decades. It began centuries ago, and if you want to comprehend it, you must also understand the generations of destruction that lie behind it.

Hardly any of the social, political, military, and religious battles that dominate our day began in our day. Studying history allows you to view your world with perception and perspective.

Next I must recommend an area where I am embarrassingly short of expertise, and I am confessing as much so that you can avoid my discomfort. Take a course in economics, at least an introduction to the subject, and perhaps one more course in microeconomics or macroeconomics. I never did, and I as yet feel doltish when discussion turns to financial matters.

What is deflation? Why is it a threat? What is the Federal Reserve? And what does it do? Why are interest rates important? What is a recession? What is a "subprime mortgage"? Or a "credit crunch"?

Don't think that only bankers and brokers ruminate on these matters. Indeed, probably no field of study impacts individual lives more directly than does economics, and I don't understand nearly enough.

You're probably thinking that had I any motivation, I'd pick up a textbook and learn what I'm missing. My failure, though, is evidence of what I've claimed all along: mastering complicated material outside school is hard. Over the years I've picked up random information about money matters, but hit-and-miss learning isn't the same as studying a subject under the discipline of an academic environment.

I also suggest that you take a course in government or "political science," as it's known on many campuses. How do the executive, legislative, and judicial branches relate to one another? How does the Supreme Court function? Why do we have federal, state, and municipal governments? How did our distinctive system come into being? And how does it compare with others around the world?

Even if you don't anticipate a career in public service, such questions ought to matter to you. Taking courses that discuss them could make you a more intelligent citizen. They may also inspire you to become a more involved citizen.

Many students who know nothing of psychology become taken with it after one class. Reflecting on human behavior, examining the inner drives and instincts that shape us, weighing the influences of environment and heredity, pondering the implications of words like "masculine" and "feminine": all these tasks are part of the discipline. Here is one subject you never stop studying, even after you've departed from school.

I'll conclude this section with a recommendation I usually make to my advisees, and in doing so I refer back to my own college courses in anthropology. From the start, this subject stimulated me. In the first semester, we focused on the history of our species: our relationship with other primates and the development of *Homo sapiens* through such stages as Neanderthal and Cro-Magnon. The second semester examined "primitive" tribes all over the world, and the parallels between those and our own "civilized" societies were startling. I don't know of any other subject that offers so vast a portrait of humanity.

To this day I read anthropology for fun. I know this claim sounds pretentious; nevertheless, that's what I do. I can add that advisees who have taken anthropology report that they found it informative and enjoyable. I shall also note that before coming to college, I knew nothing about the field. That I was required to take it gave me an introduction to what has become a lifelong diversion.

At the beginning of this section, I noted that courses in the social sciences can be demanding. But we're concerned with the quality of your education, and these subjects are difficult to handle by yourself. After graduation you may read novels, listen to a Beethoven symphony, and visit an art museum. But will you study economic theory or comparative political ideologies? The opportunity to do so is one reason you're at college.

The Sciences

We now arrive at the division about which I know least. I never had much success in science. After high-school biology, at which I was moderately successful, and high-school chemistry, at which I was less impressive, I flopped. You might recall that earlier I mentioned that I began college as a premed. Yes, I, too, had illusions. Almost immediately, however, I realized my folly and moved elsewhere.

Thus this section of the chapter will be the briefest, for I'm aware that if you plan to study science, you're going to take these courses without my urging. I'm also aware that unless science is your major field, you'll probably never take any of them, unless your college requires such selection. Otherwise most humanities and social science majors will never enter a science lab, except to wave at a friend hunched over a test tube or frog dissection. I won't be pollyannaish about this tendency, and I know that little I say will change your mind. Still, I stand by my advice. Study science. Study all you can.

I'm not advocating that you take the most advanced courses, but I do ask you to try introductory classes in at least two of the three major subjects: biology, chemistry, and physics. Almost every school offers beginning sections, probably in conjunction with multihour lab sessions. Most colleges also offer versions for nonscientists, and in your position I'd tell myself to take a couple. These days the world is simply too science-oriented for me to dally in ignorance.

Think of all the areas of human activity that you will understand better: genetics, medical and chemical research, astrophysics, and the endless array of environmental matters. You might not become expert, but at least you'll have insight into what's happening around you. Never forget, either, that the career you choose and that you think entirely independent of science may one day overlap with some of these fields.

Science courses are also beneficial in that they enlighten nonspecialists as to the nature and scope of scientific investigation. To attempt an experiment on your own is to appreciate the scientific method in a way that no reading from a textbook can provide.

Mathematics is similarly a stumbling block for many people. At the risk of further personal humiliation, I'll reveal that after breezing through elementary algebra, I went downhill, mathematically speaking. When the question concerned a certain amount of candy at one price, and how many pounds would be equivalent to that amount at another price, I was in clover. I could help everyone devise candy prices. But when the problem had anything to do with a graph, or when the realm of irrational numbers and other sophisticated concepts appeared, I faded. The more math you take, though, the better you'll be prepared for a world in which so many fields are dependent on mathematical skills.

My last recommendation is probably unnecessary. Computer courses weren't available when I was in school, but then neither were personal computers. Had such a subject existed, I suspect that even I, as nonmechanical as I am, would have pursued it. I can't think of a single contemporary career that's not in some way involved with, even dependent on, computer skills, so a grounding in the essentials is vital. These days you probably arrive at college sufficiently adept to send mail, surf the web, and download, among countless other capabilities. If not, many schools require you to learn before you graduate, and here's one requirement I assume you'll want to fulfill. Learning to move beyond the elementary stages with the computer may not be easy. Indeed, some students grapple mightily, but few deny that the effort is worthwhile.

Don't be fooled, however, into thinking that mastery of the computer will solve all academic problems. A foolish idea typed into a computer is still a foolish idea.

Of all the courses in the curriculum, those in science and mathematics may be the most formidable to laypersons. Most people assume that without extensive background they can manage poetry or American history. But science and math have a mystique. Supposedly, if you have the talent, they can be assimilated. If not, they're beyond comprehension.

Try, anyway. To prepare for life.

SUMMING UP

I've omitted many subjects: sociology, religion, geology, business, and others. I've mentioned only some that mattered deeply to me and that I'm aware have influenced my students. I'll add now that the entire curriculum is of value, depending on your aspirations and tastes.

Nonetheless, my central thesis stands. No matter what your major, no matter how you envision yourself later in life, you're at college to sample as much as possible, to achieve, in the classic phrase, "a liberal education."

Here I'll try to allay a general apprehension about unfamiliar courses. You may want to attempt one in Shakespeare, European history, or biology, but worry that a poor grade will besmirch your overall record. Remember, though, that most schools allow you to take courses "pass-fail." According to this provision, you don't receive a traditional grade, only a P or an F, or an S or a U, which stand for "satisfactory" and "unsatisfactory." You're expected to attend classes and complete all assignments, but you needn't compete with majors for As and Bs. What you seek is mastery of the fundamentals, and you'll also gain appreciation for those who do specialize. And maybe, just maybe, you'll discover that you're more gifted than you thought. Then you can take another course or two without the safety net of pass-fail.

One warning, though. Too many pass-fail courses on a transcript look unimpressive, so if your school doesn't place a limit on them, set your own. One a year is about right.

Don't, however, ignore the option. With it, you have no reason to avoid any department. The entire curriculum is yours. Enjoy it.

~~⌒

A couple of concluding thoughts.

I've met many freshmen who initially could not decide what courses to take. Nothing appealed, and our first advising session ended with their wondering how they would ever find enough to graduate.

By the middle of that same year, these same students were grabbing classes right and left, frustrated that they would never be able to take all they wanted. Time and opportunity fly by, and the four years often become too short. I expect you'll feel that same way.

My intention has been to work you into something of a dither. Yet I must offer a cautionary note. Don't proceed as though you have the responsibility to take every course in every department. There's too much to learn. Indeed, the more you learn, the more you will realize how much more you have to learn.

Don't try to acquire all human knowledge by taking eight classes at once. If the standard load is four per semester, take four. If the load is five, take five. Retain enthusiasm, but don't drive yourself mad.

Now to the next step. How do you pick courses within the bounds we've outlined? Do you choose at random, with your eye on seeking knowledge in every area? Or should a more specific strategy be applied?

I've heard of one student who went through college taking classes that met only on Tuesdays and Thursdays. Between ten and two. On the first floor.

I trust you are prepared to be more flexible. Thus as you leaf through the listings, you observe that they are taught by individuals who bear the imposing title "professor."

Who are these people?

Chapter Five

The Faculty

AN OVERALL VIEW

Near the beginning or the end of your college catalogue you will come across a compendium of names, each followed by degrees and a title, and you'll probably figure that together these men and women constitute a powerful aggregate of knowledge.

Well, the sum of learning on a university faculty is impressive. The unavoidable truth, however, is that not every one of these people is a classroom dynamo.

Years ago, a friend of mine was appointed to her first college teaching position, and almost at once became nervous that she wouldn't be able to handle it. "How do I keep the students interested?" she asked. "I'm not sure I know enough." I suggested that when she visited the campus ahead of time, she sit in on a class or two and watch some of her future colleagues in action.

Upon her return, I asked how everything went. "Well, I saw one guy," she reported, "and all he did was read from his book. He didn't raise his head the entire period. A couple of students waved their hands, but he didn't notice, so after a while no one bothered trying to say anything."

I then inquired if she was still nervous.

"A little. But I figure I have to do better than that."

Lest you think that story unique, let me quote from a course evaluation book written by students at one campus (not mine). Most schools have a version of such a publication, a compilation of judgments, usually online, intended to guide registering students. The web, too, offers sites that encompass nearly every undergraduate and graduate institution in the country. These profiles are not infallible, but some are devastating.

Here's one: "The professor has the habit of mumbling through lectures which are probably better unheard. His lectures are trivial, dull, pointless, and unimaginative."

Here's another: "One is forced to question his dedication to the course. Students say he is not very accessible for consultation. He marks exams quickly and inaccurately. His exams are vague. He answers questions inadequately, and class discussion is generally not valuable."

Inspiring words, right? The sad reality is that every college and university has instructors who receive such unflattering reports.

On the other hand, many professors receive glowing praise about their expertise, energy, and devotion. These instructors are the ones you want to find.

To appreciate them fully, you should understand the preparation that leads to a college teaching career. It takes place in graduate school, where aspiring scholars earn their doctorates or, more officially, their Ph.D.s. This abbreviation stands for "Doctor of Philosophy," which sounds as if it ought to be awarded only to those who study philosophy. In fact, it is the highest degree in just about every field.

In graduate school, the focus is on mastery of the subject. By taking courses, passing exams, and finally writing a book-length dissertation, the professor-to-be strives toward a single goal: to demonstrate command of the discipline. The program usually lasts four or five years, although finishing the dissertation may take longer.

What is seldom discussed in graduate school is the art of teaching. The unspoken assumption is that once an individual has control of the intellectual content of a subject, the rest comes naturally. Rarely is advice offered on such basic matters as how to structure a course, compose an exam, correct a paper, lead a discussion, or present a lecture.

You might think these tasks natural for those who have spent their lives in school observing teachers both good and bad, but the process doesn't follow that way. Watching teachers and being a teacher are distinct experiences.

Moreover, most people change when they move from the student side of the desk to the teacher side, a transformation that occurs at every level, not just at college. Teachers sometimes forget that students have other interests, problems, and obligations; that only a limited amount of information can be absorbed in a class period; and that a great deal of time outside class may be needed for material to be written or read. In short, teachers may forget what a student's life is like.

Elementary and secondary instructors are less likely to maintain this attitude for long, because they are under the scrutiny of parents and administrators. Thus the quality of classroom performance, and by that I mean the students' level of achievement, is all-important. If it doesn't meet a school's standard, the teacher is held responsible and expected to compensate.

Rarely, however, does anyone check on college teachers. We'll soon consider methods for evaluation, but for the most part, if college teachers ever learn, and the great ones surely do, they learn on the job.

PUBLISH OR PERISH

You may have heard this phrase. It has several implications.

The first and most important is the crucial distinction between university teachers and those elsewhere. Instructors below the college level may produce scholarship, but such activity is not compulsory. For professors, though, it is a major obligation. For many, it is *the* major obligation, so that classes and students run a distant second.

Once you arrive at college, you will soon notice that teachers here spend far less time actually instructing than do their counterparts at other types of institutions. High-school teachers present four or five classes a day, five days a week. College teachers may teach nine or even three *hours* a week. Not a day. *A week.* Twelve hours is considered a very heavy load.

Class time must be supplemented by office hours, usually a couple per week. In addition, each field imposes certain demands unique to the subject. A science professor, for instance, may supervise multihour labs. So may a foreign-language teacher. Finally, almost all instructors prepare classes and correct papers, responsibilities that vary according to experience and subject. A history teacher offering a course for the first time might need several hours to prepare for a single session, while an English professor, even one with vast experience, may spend days reviewing a set of term papers.

Yet such labors are usually completed at the professor's convenience. I perform most of mine in a large stuffed chair in my living room, and if I feel like pausing, then resuming later that day, or at night, or the following morning, no one orders me to do otherwise.

College teachers are also granted extensive vacations. Semesters here are shorter than those in high school, so winter, spring, and summer breaks are long. Furthermore, professors are periodically given paid terms away from teaching called "sabbaticals."

You should know as well that professorial salaries are not especially high. Superstars at wealthy universities may earn more than two hundred thousand dollars a year, but many regulars earn less than half that, and beginners half again. You'll argue, perhaps, that given the number of hours during which we perform our job, greater reward would be inequitable, but in comparison with others who have invested so much money in their education, like doctors, lawyers, and engineers, professors earn small financial recompense.

What we receive instead is time to conduct our own research, and thereafter to proffer those aforementioned contributions to scholarly life.

These take primarily three forms. One, professors gather frequently for symposia, where speakers read papers on matters of professional import. Two, thousands of scholarly journals appear all over the globe, and an article or review, especially in an elite publication, is a worthy accomplishment. Society outside academia may be unaware of these journals, but inside they carry considerable prestige. Three, professors write books, often published by university presses that support scholarly output not intended for a mass audience.

Are all academic papers, articles, and books contributive? Of course not. Some papers are forgotten immediately upon their single hearing, while quite a few articles and books are relegated to library shelves where they only gather dust. On the other hand, a portion of scholarly achievement influences thinking throughout a discipline, while certain monumental works do nothing less than alter our view of the world.

For teachers who publish extensively, one reward is professional eminence. Their schools are proud, and colleagues throughout the discipline grant homage. No matter how successful a professor becomes, the desire to receive such tribute remains unflagging. All scholars are proud to augment their résumés, known in academic circles as the "curriculum vitae," and thus all are delighted to speak, publish, and otherwise contribute to the discourse of our time.

For young academicians, however, scholarly achievement offers not only these returns, but one even more valuable. It is called "tenure."

TENURE

Tenure is the line of demarcation in academic life. It is the barrier that separates senior faculty from junior, and serenity from tension. It is a barrier of which everyone is conscious. Scholarly attainment is satisfying and worthwhile, but without the prize of tenure, such triumph may leave a bitter taste.

Tenure is, to put the matter bluntly, lifetime job security. After a period of time at one school, usually six years, a junior faculty member is eligible for tenure. If the candidate's department approves, and if the administration concurs, the teacher may count on a position at that school until retirement. If tenure is denied, the teacher begins packing.

The absolute nature of tenure places intense pressure upon all concerned, for the decision determines the paths of not only careers but lives.

For the last forty years, college teaching positions have been at a premium, and two or three hundred applicants for a single post are commonplace. Thus failing to gain tenure at one institution may mean not simply leaving that school and joining another, but exiting academic life altogether. And after such extensive professional study as I have described, this directive can be shattering.

When tenure is awarded, the position belongs to that teacher permanently. Unless the school undergoes catastrophic financial hardship, the only way tenured faculty can be dismissed is by committing a serious breach of ethics, and even then the accused may bring to the defense a battery of legal maneuvers that make firing so costly that many institutions are reluctant to pursue such an end. Thus tenure is the equivalent of a twenty-five- or thirty-year bond between teacher and school.

Tenure decisions are based on several criteria. The first is publications, and here's where the "perish" in "publish or perish" appears. The gist is that college teachers who fail to write scholarly material of sufficient quality, quantity, or both may find themselves out of a job. Complicating the situation is that a list of publications which would assure tenure at one school might be far less convincing at another.

How fair is any standard? A great many in the profession believe, as I do, that a teacher who writes is a teacher who thinks. Even if a book or an article is not a scholarly landmark, the very process of writing about critical issues, then presenting the results for the scrutiny of experts, is an indication that teacher is willing to grow. And with all that time away from teaching, a large percentage of professors have opportunity for such effort.

The second element that enters into the tenure decision is quality of teaching, and here's where you, the student, are asked to participate. Department members may observe classes to see the candidate in action, but colleagues also weigh evaluations that you complete at the end of each course.

Some faculty members don't mind these forms. Quite a few do.

If evaluations consisted of no more than practical information about whether the teacher returned papers promptly or showed up for office hours, most instructors wouldn't object. Frequently, however, evaluations ask students to comment on the teacher's knowledge and presentation of the material. With all respect, you're not in a position to make such assessments intelligently. You've never taken the course before; indeed, you might be altogether new to the subject. And often what sounds to you like stunning insight may be superficiality.

Such evaluations also put junior faculty in the awkward position of needing the good will of those they are to judge. You know that a teacher who gives you high grades is apt to rise in your estimation. Thus an untenured instructor who awards low grades risks receiving damaging reviews from resentful students, a state of affairs that threatens the integrity of the educational process.

To return to tenure. The two major factors that enter into a departmental decision are publications and teaching. A third, service to the school, usually in the form of committee work, is last and least.

Yet the question remains: what importance is given to each component? How, for instance, does a department treat a brilliant teacher who has written little? A successful scholar who's a dud in the classroom? Someone only adequate in both areas who has given vital service to the college? What happens to someone enthusiastically praised by the department, but thought second-rate by the administration? Every case is different, and standards vary from school to school, department to department, and individual to individual. Furthermore, as impartial as these decisions should be, they may be complicated by political and personal antagonism, professional prejudice and jealousy, and other sources of discord. Furthermore, the outcomes can arouse great bitterness, and enmities that last for a lifetime often originate in a tenure decision.

Since the system is fraught with problems, you may wonder why tenure even exists. Virtually all other professions survive without bestowing lifetime security on certain members. What makes professors special?

Because tenure guarantees academic freedom. And nowhere is freedom of speech and thought more vital than at a university, which by its very name suggests that it will tolerate all points of view. At a university, no idea should be so dangerous that it cannot be discussed. Now more than ever, when special-interest groups from every side of the political and social spectrum insist that professors be punished for expressing controversial opinions, tenure affirms our freedom to write and speak without fear of retribution.

Sad to say, the consequences of tenure are not always beneficial. Sometimes the unfortunate does occur, and a school is stuck with a slacker who fulfills classroom and scholarly responsibilities minimally, if at all. Such figures frustrate everyone, supporters and opponents of tenure alike.

On the other hand, many professors thrive under the banner of tenure. It allows them to offer intellectually adventurous teaching and publishing that make a genuine contribution to their students, their school, and, on occasion, their society. For that reason, the tenure system, whatever its flaws, must not be abandoned.

ACADEMIC STRATA

I've offered an overview of professors and their way of life. In doing so, and throughout this book, I've used *professor*, *teacher*, and *instructor* interchangeably, and before long I'll revert to that style. For the moment, though, let me differentiate between official categories.

At the top of the heap are professors, sometimes called "full professors." They are the most senior members, they almost invariably have tenure, and they probably have had it for years. They are also the most experienced members of the faculty, veterans of a particular campus, and the most powerful political forces both within their own departments and throughout the school. They teach whatever courses they choose, and often carry the lightest classroom load.

The next level is that of associate professors, who also usually have tenure. In fact, the honor is often accompanied by the title. Although they have less seniority than full professors, and still seek that final promotion, they generally teach what they want. They also have political clout in that they can vote on future candidates for tenure.

Next we enter the realm of junior faculty, who, we must clarify immediately, do *not* have tenure. They have less choice about what they teach, and frequently take on courses that demand heavy correcting and other time-consuming activity. Among these are many introductory classes.

We begin with assistant professors. Almost all have their doctorates, so their minds are preoccupied with one goal: tenure.

Assistant professors may be divided into two categories: those on "tenure-track lines" and those with "terminal contracts." The tenure-track line indicates that the assistant professor has a multiyear contract and, if all goes well, will become a candidate for tenure. A terminal contract is just as ominous as it sounds. Once the contract ends, the professor should not expect to be reappointed.

Whether an assistant professor is on tenure track is clarified at the initial appointment, and the decision is based primarily on how the teacher's areas of expertise, which may be needed during a particular term, match department priorities as anticipated for years to come. Lines, however, may be added or dropped at any time, so no assistant professor's status is safe.

Below the rank of assistant professor are those who bear titles like "instructor," "lecturer," "associate," and "assistant." These individuals have yet to conclude their graduate work. The stumbling block is usually the doctoral dissertation, that book-length manuscript that may take years to complete. Those in this category are frequently branded "ABD" (all-but-dissertation), and often try to coordinate teaching with finishing their doctorates, never a trouble-free task.

This outline should clarify differences in rank among the faculty. Just as we occasionally forget that you belong to different classes, so you may ignore our distinct plateaus.

We don't.

EVALUATING TEACHERS

Now you're aware that teachers have a lot on their minds, a lot that has nothing to do with you. Given all this information, what steps should you take?

You may conclude as follows: "I'd better grab all the full and associate professors I can, and leave the junior faculty to the losers."

That system won't do. Seniority is no guarantee of classroom competence.

"Oh," you say, "then I'll look for the famous scholars. They publish a lot, and I'm sure I'll learn from a teacher who knows so much."

That plan won't suffice, either. Scholarship and teaching ability are not necessarily complementary.

"Then I'll go for the young ones. At least they'll be close to my age, and we might be good friends."

Sorry. Youth ensures neither enthusiasm nor amiability.

In fact, I can't give you one description that encompasses the best teachers, because one doesn't exist. At every school and level you will find inspiring and dedicated teachers. Some will be veterans; some will be newcomers. Some will be world famous; some will be local personalities. Great teachers come in all varieties. So do less helpful pedagogues.

Remember, too, that all good teachers are not alike, and what's fine for someone else may be all wrong for you, and vice versa. You probably recall one teacher in high school who was a favorite of yours, but whom your friends thought dull or demanding. Tastes differ.

You may need or enjoy a teacher who's full of energy, who speaks loudly and bustles about the room. Or you may prefer a pensive soul with a more soft-spoken approach, who offers hardly any theatrics.

You may need a teacher who drives the class hard, who's willing to call on and even embarrass students to keep everyone alert. Or you may recoil at such coercion, and appreciate a teacher who lets you reflect on material without being singled out for response.

You may prefer a teacher who mostly lectures, or one who encourages regular discussion. You may enjoy a teacher who peppers the class with jokes and stories, or one who sticks to the material and permits no distractions.

All of these teachers can present organized, enjoyable, and intellectually stimulating courses. Choose the best for you.

As you conduct this search, however, keep in mind that almost all of us in academic life recall a teacher who helped shape us. I suspect the same is true for most people outside academia. You, too, may have already benefited from such a figure in high school, junior high, or even elementary school.

At college you will meet many more teachers. Not all will have lasting impact, but a few will have a profound and positive influence, and they're a major reason why you're here. Try hard to find them. You can't put your energy to better use.

Chapter Six

Creating Your Program

PRELIMINARY THINKING

Let's review. You've arrived at school and settled in. You know your reasons for coming and your long-range goals. You're eager to choose useful courses in a variety of disciplines. In other words, you're prepared to register.

The main challenge here is that you must juggle several factors simultaneously: schoolwide requirements as well as those in a possible major, electives that satisfy your own demands for the education you want, and the best teachers. You also have to try to arrange the entire package into a schedule that fits how you want to run your life.

At times your vision will have to be modified. But for now let's put aside that worry, and think idealistically.

MAKING CHOICES

This section will be brief, for we've already considered the task in depth.

I'll assume that in front of you is a list of classes. Don't look at the catalogue to find out what's available. Check the offerings and instructors for the immediate semester. When you're a freshman, go to the registrar or online and locate the current master schedule. You can then carry out all the advice that follows, except that you'll have to move quickly, since the academic year will start soon. Still, you have the orientation period as well as a day or two before the actual opening, so don't panic.

I noted earlier that the college may have provided you with a program. Use this as a framework, but don't be bound by it.

Now, with all course listings at hand, set out before yourself, and perhaps before your advisor, the schoolwide requirements. Then divide them over your first few semesters, so that you can see how you might complete them efficiently. Don't pile on so many that you choke yourself academically, but don't dawdle, either. Give yourself a reasonable target.

Decide, for instance, that by the end of your sophomore year you will have taken all courses necessary for your degree. That plan will introduce you to most of the college curriculum and leave you two full years to explore.

Next, if you have the faintest idea of a major, look for an introductory course in that subject. If it turns out to be the right one, you're on your way to completing the responsibility. If you change your mind, you can start over. During each semester, try to take at least one subject that could count in your area of concentration.

Lastly, if you have room, search out a useful elective.

When making out this program, try to maintain an overview of the entire four years. Ask yourself how each course you anticipate taking will contribute to your general education.

Then move to the next step.

FINDING THE RIGHT TEACHERS

The preceding chapter should have left you with the impression that the most important component of any course is the instructor. You're right. I steadfastly maintain that your number-one priority is ensuring as best you can that the people who for the next fourteen weeks will be speaking before you and grading your work are folks you respect and like.

The primary way to find good teachers is to ask. Other students will be happy to regale you with stories and opinions, and after you check all sources, certain names will loom large. Furthermore, as we have mentioned, students at your school may publish candid comments about faculty. Whether or not such information is available openly, gather as much as possible.

Remember in your investigation not to limit yourself to a favorite subject or area. No field is intrinsically dull or interesting. Presentation is the key.

A bad teacher can make you hate any subject in a week. A great teacher can inspire you to love a subject for life.

Keep these axioms in mind especially when registering for required courses, because the right professor can make even these classes favorites.

The same principle applies to courses that you're sure you'll enjoy. Let's say you've always been interested in politics, and you come across a class titled "The American Political System." Sounds perfect, right? When you make inquiries, however, you discover that the person offering the subject this semester has published a well-received book, but that otherwise no one has a positive word for him.

Then someone tells you about an incredible professor who teaches medieval history. At first you're reluctant. Medieval history does not sound spiffy. Still, everyone tells you that this woman, who hasn't written much, is a force in the classroom, and students pack her lectures.

Which course do you take?

The choice is clear, I hope. Read the other guy's book, but take medieval history. If you sign up for politics, at least when that fellow is teaching it, you may end up suffering through a woeful semester. Medieval history, on the other hand, may turn out to be gripping.

The dilemma I've just dramatized was easy to resolve. Others aren't so simple. You shouldn't sign up for just any teachers who happen to be popular. Ask why they're popular.

When I was an undergraduate, one new man quickly gained distinction by giving everyone in his sociology section a straight A. No matter how students did on papers and exams, all earned an A. The next semester his classes were mobbed, as everyone wanted that sure A, except by then the instructor had decided to change his reputation, and gave everyone a D.

Don't choose teachers because they're supposed to be entertaining or easy. Choose teachers who are reputed to offer worthwhile courses.

FINDING THE RIGHT COURSES

Let's assume you're intrigued by a particular class because of either the teacher's reputation or the catalogue description. Don't be bashful about visiting the professor or the department assistant and asking to peruse the syllabus. It will tell a lot.

First, see how much reading will be assigned per week. If the professor intends to cover a thousand pages, note that information. Remember, the professor has read the texts; thus for him (we'll assume this one's a man) the load may seem light. For you, that number may be impossible.

How many written assignments will you have to turn out? Suppose the instructor (this one's a woman) expects you to write one paper a week, each six to eight pages. She may think that number reasonable. Then again, she won't be writing the papers.

I don't want you to steer clear of teachers who demand a lot. Just be aware of the distinction between a challenging series of assignments and a preposterous one. If a good teacher offers a course that you know will be beneficial but tough, you should want to take it. The instructors to avoid are those with no understanding of the burdens their assignments impose.

Check whether class participation is required. If the syllabus indicates that everyone will be expected to present regular oral reports, and you're someone who's delighted to hold forth in front of groups, maybe you've found a home. If, on the other hand, you find speaking in class an ordeal, decide whether now is the time that you want to confront with your phobia.

See whether the course has prerequisites. In other words, does the teacher expect you to enter the class with substantial background? This problem often occurs with language courses, where, for instance, the word "intermediate" means different things to different people.

Does the instructor expect regular attendance? Some teachers decree that more than two absences from their course guarantees failure. Some teachers do not accept late papers, so that a submission that arrives any time after the deadline receives an automatic F. Decide if you can live according to such strictures.

The class syllabus should provide most of this information. Other students will fill in the rest.

Now let's take the process of registration one step further. Suppose you know of an excellent teacher who's offering one section of a large course divided into several such sections. Find that teacher and ask to join his or her class. You may be rebuffed, told that you'll have to accept wherever you're assigned. If so, you're no worse off than when you started. On the other hand, some teachers will try to help you.

Don't think that I'm asking you merely to curry favor. You're investing a great deal of time and money in your college education. Making the most of it means working with the best teachers you can find.

Let's imagine that a course you want has a prerequisite of another you haven't taken. Yet you're confident you can handle the subject. Visit the instructor and ask for permission to register. Official prerequisites can usually be modified or eliminated if the instructor is willing, and many are, if you express interest.

One hazard that proves especially frustrating is enrollment limits, usually decreed by a department seeking to make sure that their class rosters are of roughly equal size. A few may be necessitated by the seating capacity of the assigned room.

Years ago, students used to queue up hours early in hope of ensuring that their selections remained open. These days, however, registration is usually carried out online, so you are spared that indignity. Nonetheless, the process often follows in sequence, with upperclassmen having first choice, so by the time you're permitted to link into the system, certain courses may be full. In that case, try to put yourself on the waiting list, then show up for the first session of the semester, when most teachers will accept you.

If this roll of extra names is also closed, don't give up. Contact the professor and ask if he or she allows more students than the announced maximum. If the answer is affirmative, attend on the first day, and again chances are that you'll be fine. For security's sake, sign up for something else, then drop it when the right course opens.

Even if the professor rejects your petition, however, I still urge you to show up on that first day. Students leave courses all the time, and a vacancy might appear just when you do. Besides, once you're standing in the room, and you and the professor both see empty seats, only a churlish soul will deny you. If such is the case, don't feel bad. You're probably better off with someone else.

CONSTRUCTING YOUR SCHEDULE

We're ready for the next step: selecting classes according to the times offered.

This privilege sounds like fun, and I suspect I know what you're thinking. After years of waking up and immediately scrambling off to school, you're determined to avoid early-morning classes. You want time to sleep, so that if you stay up late to work or socialize, you can recover.

Your plans may have to be modified if the course you want meets at 8:00 a.m. Then you'll have to decide which is more valuable: your comfort or your education.

Another aspect of early classes deserves mention. One of the peculiarities of college life, indeed, of life altogether, is that if you don't work in the morning when you're fresh, you're likely to waste that morning.

Here you might object, claiming that you are one of those people who functions better at night. Or early, early in the morning. Like 3:00 a.m., after unwinding for a while.

Possibly.

All I ask is that you schedule classes according to the right emphasis. For some people, waking up for an 8:00 a.m. session is impossible. Quite a few more people talk themselves into believing that they are ineffective at that hour. For most of us, however, early classes are a help. Indeed, whatever gets you up and moving is a help. The longer you doze, the more time you waste.

What I've just written may sound hopelessly stiff-necked, something in the spirit of "early to bed and early to rise" (especially when I confess that I myself teach during those early-morning hours). My apologies. But the point stands. Don't plan your college education around your pleasures. You'll have plenty anyway. Schedule classes so that you give yourself the best chance for learning. If the right ones meet in the afternoon, fine. If some meet earlier, even much earlier, don't avoid them.

Besides, most extracurriculars, like sports and organizations, come to life in the afternoon and evening. You won't want your classes to interfere with the rest of your existence.

Don't pack all your classes into a couple of days. You may be tempted to include as many as possible on Tuesdays and Thursdays so that you can take an occasional extra-long weekend. Unless the prospect is unavoidable, though, don't plan for more than three classes on any day. By the fourth you'll be punchy. You'll also find that preparing for so many classes on a single day can become fatiguing. True, in high school each of your five or six classes met five days a week, but college classes last longer and move more intensely. Take my word: no more than three classes per day, unless circumstances demand otherwise.

You will also find yourself with the option of choosing between classes that convene two times a week and those that meet three times. The two-day courses last approximately an hour and a half. The three-day courses last about an hour.

One factor that will propel you toward two-day classes is that none meet on both Friday and Monday. You'll soon discover that for college students and faculty alike, a regular three-day weekend is a luxury that turns into a necessity.

Again, don't put ease ahead of education. If the quality instructor teaches the right course on Mondays, Wednesdays, and Fridays, don't tell yourself that going skiing is more important. Take that course.

Need I also tell you to break for lunch? Don't laugh. Some students figure that one donut in the morning with a cup of coffee, or a candy bar and a bottle of soda around noon, will sustain them for five straight class hours. Give yourself time to eat and relax. If you don't, you'll be nodding off in the middle of somewhere.

Let me conclude this chapter by noting that the ideal schedule may not work out. Nonetheless, just as teachers try to arrange their classes for maximum productivity and convenience, you're entitled to do the same. Teachers, however, need worry only about themselves. The only stipulation to which they must adjust is that all courses in their department cannot be offered in the same favored time slots.

Your task is more complex, and therefore you'll likely have to compromise. A class you want might be irrevocably closed. Two highly desirable courses might meet simultaneously. A wonderful course might meet when you have an unbreakable commitment to an extracurricular activity. Your job might preclude your taking morning or afternoon courses.

One common problem arises from laboratory sessions for science courses or studio sessions for art courses. These often require a two- or three-hour segment per week, and even when you can choose one of several sections, the rest of your schedule might have to be framed to accommodate a lengthy session.

Whatever the difficulty, you may have to settle, and the area where settling is most common is in choice of teachers. No specific instructors are required by a college or department. Specific courses are.

Thus you may end up with a teacher you don't know, or someone whose reputation is less than stellar. You may have to decide between teachers of dubious distinction. Despite your best efforts, you may end up with classes that don't work out.

That misfortune doesn't excuse you from learning. As I indicated in the first chapter, responsibility for your education rests with you, and even if the classroom part of a course falls short, you can read and study as much as you want.

I admit, however, that listless classes can be disheartening. In the face of such obstacles, all you can do is your best. So use your judgment, try to apply the guidelines we've considered, and schedule classes as intelligently as you can.

Chapter Seven

Carrying Out Your Program

You've registered, you have a schedule, and you're prepared to take on the challenges of college.

Now, I hesitate to say, comes the tough part. Fortunately you've been attending school for a long time, and you know fundamentally what to do. At college, however, conditions are different. Thus I'll offer a few suggestions about conducting yourself so as to gain the most from classes and to avoid errors that will negate good efforts elsewhere.

ATTENDING CLASS

My first reminder is so elementary that you may think it ridiculous to mention. But here it is: go to class. You can't learn anything if you don't.

In high school you probably never faced this problem. Oh, you may have cut from time to time, or at least you were tempted. But someone was taking attendance, and you had to weigh the possible consequences of absence. That pressure probably kept you going on occasions when you were leaning the other way.

Some professors take attendance. At larger colleges and universities, though, virtually no one does, for classes are usually too populous for the teacher to spend time calling the names. Besides, most instructors are grateful for any reason not to bother.

I don't take attendance. Not that I don't care who's present, for I'm conscious of who is and who isn't. I just don't take official action. My students have paid for the course. If they don't want to show up, or if they have another priority, they ought to be allowed to exercise their own judgment.

Perhaps I sound callous, but I don't believe I am. I do believe that leading your own life is both one of the privileges and one of the learning experiences at college. I like to think I give my students all the assistance I can, but I don't run after them, begging to help. You have the right to make mistakes, and if I take attendance, I'm robbing you of some responsibility. I do, however, give frequent and unannounced quizzes, and I don't give makeups. Thus I provide motivation of a different sort.

Let me add that cutting is a habit easily acquired, because so many more alluring activities are available. What sometimes led me astray, and you'll probably think I'm either kidding or remarkably dull, was the chess club, where I used to go after lunch. Often I found myself playing right until class, and just as often I was eager to continue. One day my opponent mentioned that I kept looking at my watch. When I explained why, he kindly pushed me out. He had recognized the danger signs.

I don't want to become melodramatic. Playing chess hardly left me in a state of moral and physical debilitation. Nonetheless, the principle applies.

During class hours, all sorts of distractions will surface. Some will be constructive: working on the newspaper, preparing for another course, or helping a friend pack and move. Some will be useless: chatting in the dining hall or . . . well, you fill in the rest. But you belong in class. Even if one class has not lived up to your hopes, even if it is not exciting or informative, go.

Certain colleagues might warn you about attending when you have not completed the day's assignment, for supposedly you will run the risk of being called on and having your inadequacies exposed. Ignore this advice. Unless you are sure that you will be singled out and that the teacher will be peeved when you don't know an answer, get there, if only to help yourself catch up. If you neglect the reading, don't compound your dereliction.

As long as you're going, be on time. Few things annoy a professor or other students more than intruders who traipse in five or ten minutes late. Not only do they interrupt the proceedings; they also must stumble through the maze of desks, simultaneously kicking satchels and knocking books to the floor.

Remember, too, that some professors (like yours truly) begin classes promptly. Indeed, I always give quizzes, distribute assignments, and make announcements within the first several minutes. Most of my students quickly grasp my habitude and arrive on time, but the rare latecomer always misses something.

Let me conclude this section by noting that cutting class is at times unavoidable. You may have a personal obligation that demands immediate attention, or you may be so ill that staying in bed or going to the infirmary is the only recourse. Don't, however, talk yourself into such a condition. If you miss class, the reason should be compelling.

If you are absent, and if the class is small enough (let's say under fifty) that the vacancy will be apparent, take the first opportunity to explain why. The teacher will respect your maturity, and you'll feel more like an adult. If you know beforehand that you will have to cut because of a campus appointment, a job interview, or a family commitment, speak up. Teachers are human. We understand these matters.

Most of us do, that is. Be prepared for the instructor who won't excuse you for intramural soccer or your cousin's wedding. If you find yourself under the jurisdiction of someone who doesn't accept absence or lateness, you face a quandary. Are the course and teacher worth that kind of pressure? Are you someone who occasionally needs a break?

Don't figure the teacher will make an exception for you. One of my advisees took a course with a professor who announced on the first day that a single unexcused lateness or absence would mean automatic failure. Weeks into the semester, my advisee, who at the time had an A average in the course, was two minutes late because she had helped another student with a personal problem. The next morning I received a note informing me that my student had been told to drop the class. If she didn't, she would receive an F. I urged my colleague to reconsider, but he was adamant.

(Just so you don't remain in a state of high dudgeon, let me add that after the details of the crisis came to light, the lateness was classified as "excused." Many other students of the same instructor were not so fortunate.)

College teachers are an independent lot. Just as you are allowed to come and go as you wish, so we are allowed to establish policies that are as rigid as we want. Don't ever assume that we shall suspend our rules to accommodate you. You have to adjust in this world, insufferable though that process can be. College is a place to start.

IN CLASS

This section may appear unnecessary, but you'd be amazed how many people disregard commonsense classroom strategies. I repeat again that in high school these students were told what to do. Now that they are in college, they exercise their freedom in the most bizarre ways, managing to waste their own time and concurrently to antagonize both teachers and colleagues.

First, bring the text. Needless advice, you say? A percentage in every class fails to adhere to it.

Imagine for a moment that you're the instructor, and you announce that you'd like to begin on page 158. Everyone turns to page 158. Everyone, that is, except those members who haven't bothered to bring the book. They sit staring, as if to say, "I'll do it my way, when and how I want."

You're the teacher. What do you think?

Now you're a student again. Leave aside your apparent contempt for the course, the teacher, and other students. If everyone else is discussing page 158 and you don't have it, you're lost. When you finally deign to study, you'll have forgotten all about page 158.

Meanwhile everyone's looking at page 158, and you're not. What do you do? You play with your pen (if you bothered to bring one). You practice your signature. You stare into space. What you're not doing is concentrating and following. On the other hand, if you participate in the activities of the class, you'll learn more. That's why you should bring a notebook. I don't care what kind, although the old-fashioned loose-leaf may be too bulky for college desks. Try spirals, perhaps one for each course. In any case, supply yourself with paper and a writing implement.

Sounds simple, doesn't it? Who wouldn't know to bring a notebook or the text? Lots of people, including some very bright students who for reasons of their own figure that in college the old rules don't apply.

Whatever the cause, these folks turn into tourists. They take in sights and sounds, but they learn next to nothing, and they contribute less.

I recognize that for some of you money is tight, while texts grow ever more expensive. In that case, try to find a used copy, which will cost less and may be in fine condition. It may also have useful underlining courtesy of a previous reader. If no used copy is available, search for the book in the library. Perhaps you can borrow it from a friend taking the same course in a different section. All I'm asking is that you make an effort. If you absolutely cannot obtain a copy, at least look on with the person next to you.

Don't just sit there. Do something.

Except eating. Please remember that classrooms are not cafeterias. No professor wants to conduct business in the face of someone munching a tuna sandwich. Or something more ostentatious. I remember a young woman who took her accustomed seat in the front row of one of my Shakespeare classes, then took out a paper bag. Just as I started discussing *Hamlet*, she pulled out a bunch of grapes, tilted her head back, and dropped one grape, then another, into her mouth. At this point I stopped speaking and simply stared. Within seconds, she became aware of the silence surrounding her and sat up straight. "Does this bother you?" she asked. I nodded. She looked surprised, then inquired, "Would you like me to put them away?" I nodded again. While the class watched in astonishment, she repacked her grapes, in apparent wonder at my fussiness.

On a more constructive note, do raise your hand from time to time. If class discussion is part of the course, teachers appreciate and respect students who respond. Your comments suggest that you keep up with the work and that you care. In terms of grades, raising your hand often has benefits.

A more important reason for participating is that when you do, you automatically become involved. You listen more intently to rejoinders, and you remember material better. When you sit and say nothing, you tend to dream and lose contact.

Accept this advice from someone who never raised his hand. As a student, I squirmed at the thought of people watching me as I talked. Obviously in my current position I've overcome that self-consciousness, but in high school and college I said nary a word. I was the fellow sitting in the corner gazing blankly ahead. My glasses may have provided a demeanor of wisdom, but too often my expression reflected not cogitation but reverie.

Make an effort to contribute, but don't talk just to hear yourself or to create a phony impression. Such tactics are all too transparent, even to teachers. Fellow students will see through you much faster. Make points succinctly, then stop. No one, especially your colleagues, cares to hear you ramble, and the instructor who values a perceptive comment or question will lose patience if you babble endlessly.

Avoid personal reminiscence. When a professor momentarily offers a story apart from the topic, most of the class enjoys the personal touch. When a student takes off on a flight of garrulity, everyone inwardly groans.

If you have a thought you wish to expand, but sense that others have heard enough from you, speak to the teacher privately. When forty people aren't listening and waiting, your remarks are more welcome. And if what you have to say turns out to be less than insightful, no harm is done.

Some of you may be as I was, chronically shy, so that raising your hand to speak is agonizing. I always envied those students who could expatiate with assurance. By the time I reached graduate school, after teaching for a couple of years, I developed the habit of contributing at least once each class. Nothing profound, mind you: just an answer to a moderately direct question. Maybe I'd ask a question myself, although I rarely managed that gesture of originality. I found, though, and my students have confirmed my conclusion, that if you participate during every class meeting, the process becomes easier. You'll become accustomed to the sound of your voice in that environment, and you'll assume that everyone else will. Just try. If the class is small enough that discussion is important, resolve to make one comment per session. When you are in doubt as to what to say, "Could you repeat that?" will suffice.

I reiterate: you're not talking to apple-polish or whatever earthier term you prefer. You're talking to remain alert, keep your mind on the subject, and think. If the teacher values your efforts, you've done yourself some good. Best of all, when you respond, you'll enjoy classes more, even those that formerly failed to captivate you.

Remember to take notes. Don't copy every word uttered, but do jot down salient points. It's been my experience that whether you're reading on your own or following in class, citing important passages in the text is useful. Mark in pencil, so that if you make an error you don't deface the book. Underlining and otherwise noting are good ways to maintain focus.

As an example of an incompetent note-taker, I again turn to myself. As I've indicated, I indulged in more than my share of daydreaming. I kept my notebook open, but I hardly used it, except to allow my pen to drift over the page. The consequences appeared at exam time, when I found myself reviewing a collocation of doodles.

One detour.

By now you may have the impression that I was something less than an academic fireball. Such is the case. I worked hard enough to earn solid grades, so that from time to time my name appeared on honor rolls, but I wasn't as motivated as I should have been. I learned much more about succeeding as a student when I began teaching and witnessed mistakes by my charges.

Most teachers try to present an image of infallibility. We seem askance at your moments of weakness, as if we ourselves never came unprepared, never submitted a late or inadequate paper, and never floundered in any of the ways that I've been discussing. Don't be deceived. We made plenty of mistakes, but many of us also learned, and one of our aims is to help you do the same.

OUTSIDE CLASS

You're in the right class. You're attending as often as possible. You're raising your hand and participating usefully. You're taking thorough notes. Are you doing it all?

Not quite. You also have to prepare outside class.

Reading

Here is not the place for me to run down a list of study techniques, most of which you've probably heard. I can't resist, however, mentioning a few.

I hope you know not to try to work with a television or music on. Folks, you can't read Dostoevsky with rap blaring.

I hear the response: "I can, too, and I've been doing it for years." Okay. You have that out of your system. Now ask yourself honestly: can you really read and understand that way? Of course not. Half your mind, at least half, must be occupied with the noise. You're human. That's what happens to human beings. Every sensation that hits our brains absorbs part of our concentration. (I told you I was good in biology.)

You can't read, think, and listen as profitably as you can read and think in silence. Save the entertainment for when you don't have to read and think.

With all the music in the dormitory, and amid the pervasive atmosphere of revelry, your room is likely to be noisy. Friends will barge in every two minutes, and you're going to want to enjoy their company. From the hallway, certain clamorous voices will attract you, while others will distract you. In short, focusing in the dorm may be a problem. Where should you go?

Relocate in the library, a key building on campus. Chances are it will be subdued, for the tradition of whispering in a library, any library, lives on, even during peak hours. You can always find a private corner in the stacks where books are kept, where no one will disturb you, and where you can accomplish as much in one hour as you might in four in the dorm. You will also find your work of higher quality.

When in the library, relax by walking around and locating resources like magazines, journals, and newspapers on file. Reading issues from past years or decades is a relaxing and profitable way to escape momentary pressures. You may not need specific materials immediately, but effective use of the library is one of the most valuable skills you can acquire.

While there, don't hesitate to supplement assigned reading with explanatory material. Let's say the text for a course is murky. Another view of the subject from a different book may shed the right light. You won't always have time for extra reading, but if you're in the building, you might be motivated to find secondary sources. If you're back in the dorm, you'll probably acquiesce to confusion.

By the way, if you ever need a job at college, and many of you will be required to take one to fulfill scholarship obligations, try the library. The work will be orderly, and you'll learn how to use the place.

At most schools, the library remains open until late at night, so you should be able to accomplish all you want. By the time you return to the dorm, it will have quieted, so you can finish any remaining assignments, relax, or go to sleep (a novel idea).

A final piece of advice. Don't plan on studying for too long a time. You won't last. Working in several short sessions interrupted by appropriate breaks will be far more productive than forcing yourself through one marathon, the last half of which will be squandered. Better three two-hour exertions than one six-hour endurance contest.

A general word about studying. In high school you were probably prodded strongly to do your work. How many days passed by without a quiz, report, or some other measure to confirm that you were keeping up? Few, I suspect.

Not in college. Here you may go for months without any written or oral assignment. The most important skill you can acquire in college, and the one that will serve you best throughout life, is self-discipline: the capacity to work when no one looks over your shoulder. In college, hardly anyone looks.

In September of your freshman year, during the first meeting of each course, you will receive a syllabus. It will probably delineate the texts, the schedule of assignments, and the due dates for papers. Most of these will be set for the final two or three weeks of the semester, approximately when final examinations are given. Another essay or exam might be scheduled earlier, but perhaps not. The entire grade for the course may be based on as little as one or two samples of your handiwork. Therefore on those first days you'll inspect your reading lists, smile, and assume that the next couple of months should be great fun, with occasional reading tossed in. That night you'll head back to the dorm and greet your pals: "Heyyyy! I'm free 'til November. Let's go for pizza!" Then you'll head out for an evening of fun and games. By the time you return, you'll already be behind.

You may sail along in such style for quite a while. Oh, you'll make a token effort, but there's so much reading, and . . . well, nobody's watching, and you figure you can always catch up. Then in the last weeks of the semester, you face papers in every class, several exams, and a good many sleepless, panic-filled nights. You scramble to finish, drive yourself loony, and proudly proclaim that you have concluded the first term of undergraduate education. You have also managed to avoid learning anything.

At college, nothing is easier than falling behind. You can be sure that here you will be asked to undertake more reading than you would ever have believed yourself capable of doing, perhaps hundreds of pages per week. And it is oh-so-tempting to let assignments slip by while you enjoy yourself.

Don't give in.

From your first night, try to keep up. When you sit in class without having completed (or started) the assignment, you feel stupid. You also feel nervous for fear the instructor might call on you. You also understand only about a third of what's happening, and whatever concentration you muster disintegrates. Meanwhile you forget to take part in the action, in the form of either intelligent oral contributions or precise note-taking.

Are teachers aware of who's behind? Sometimes. The condition of texts may be a giveaway, because if the book hasn't been opened or has been used only a tad, its appearance says so. Thus I can usually tell who's with me and who's not, but I've been known to err on this point. Some students who have appeared in complete command were, I later learned, actually far behind. And others who seemed to be floating in the clouds were right on top of things.

Whether you're discovered or not, the inevitable result of letting reading pile up is the time-honored convention of cramming. You've probably indulged in this practice already, but never as you will at college. At the end of every semester, a couple of days are set aside as a reading period, when students jam the library, hustling to locate selections assigned during early classes. Then these individuals stuff information into themselves, trying to keep everything in order.

How successful are they? Some may triumph on exams, and score even higher than those students who have worked all semester. (I know this acknowledgement seems to sabotage my argument, but I'm being forthright.) Yet how much do these crammers ultimately learn? Not much. Material ingested steadily over weeks is material learned thoroughly. Material shoved in during several hours flows out soon after. In short, by cramming you have an outside chance of conquering the immediate exam, but you lose out on your education.

You know how you should study for a final. The time should be the culmination of effort exerted over the entire semester.

Let's fantasize for a moment. All term you've been carrying out assignments promptly, reading with pencil in hand and marking significant passages. You've affirmed how effective a reader you are when you've attended class and reviewed under the teacher's guidance, marking additional passages and adding commentary. Now, at examination time, you're rereading familiar material, devoting your energies to synthesis, gaining an overview of the semester's work, and assuring yourself that you have mastered the course.

What a magnificent picture.

Alas, for very few does education resolve so neatly. Most of us, professional academicians included, have undergone the ritual of cramming, passing, and forgetting. I also fell victim, as if this news would surprise you. The close of a semester is manic, with final papers and exams hurtling headlong. Meanwhile, so many other enterprises, like performances, exhibitions, and sports, are reaching climatic moments. The entire populace is racing around trying to maintain equilibrium. No matter how organized you are, you'll end up frazzled. The spirit is infectious.

But if you're aware of the upcoming madness, you might, during the calmer part of the term, plan ahead. When you do, you'll spare yourself infuriating and exhausting nights. You'll learn more as well. You'll also leave college with the work habits and, yes, the self-discipline, to succeed anywhere you try.

Writing

At no time is self-discipline needed more than when you write papers. Even sharp students may end up bamboozled for no other reason than a failure to anticipate upcoming projects.

Most professors provide at least a couple of weeks' notice before a paper is expected. Yet too many students wait until the last day or two to begin. Some imagine that the perfect topic will appear over the rainbow, and that the paper will thereby write itself. Folks, the perfect topic doesn't exist. All are hard. If you find a suitable subject a few weeks before the paper is expected, begin right away. If possible, finish before much longer. Then put the paper aside, and submit it on the day it's due. The tranquility that such an accomplishment affords will astound you.

I generally invite students working on papers for me to bring an early version to my office, but I'm always amazed at how many wait until the last minute to avail themselves of this offer. Let's say that four weeks ago I assigned an essay to be submitted on Thursday morning; the length is one thousand to fifteen hundred words, or approximately four to six pages. Invariably, some students saunter in on Wednesday with what they hope is a viable topic. When I hint that they're cutting matters close, they answer, no, they've set aside that night to write an outline and a draft, then revise, all by three the next morning. That's when they figure on grabbing two hours' sleep. If the paper needs further revision, they save an hour after breakfast to tinker. They admit that they also have a psychology report due by four o'clock, and they haven't started that, either, but not to worry. Everything will work out.

What amazes me is that this scheme is delineated as if it were the product of serious foresight. I'll wager some of you are thinking a version of what these students sometimes insist: "I work best under pressure, so I always leave my papers for the last night. Then I write one draft, revise, and hand it in. I do real well that way."

The genesis of this rationalization was probably a minor success from years before, when these individuals fell behind on an essay due in twelve hours and were forced to grind it out in one sitting. Through some miraculous stroke of fortune they earned a good grade, and now operate under the assumption that they thrive under insane duress.

The real lesson of the one lucky paper was that the writers, facing a severe time constraint, truly concentrated for a few hours and produced a strong effort. They could have concentrated just as hard a week before, and the paper would have been just as successful. In fact, with extra time for revision, it probably would have been better.

On other occasions, when those same students try to churn out a product in a few hours, they can't harness similar intensity, and the papers flop. Will such students alter their strategies? No. They've talked themselves into a state of mind that gives them an excuse to avoid starting ahead of time.

What makes this syndrome even more tempting is that many professors are lax about deadlines for papers. They announce a due date but fail to adhere to it. If you submit your work one day or even a few days late, they don't mind. And too often if they don't, you don't.

Other professors are more demanding and penalize lateness by lowering your grade. For instance, if the paper is expected Monday morning, and you submit it Monday afternoon, you can earn no higher grade than B. Submit it Tuesday, and you're down to a C. Some teachers follow this procedure strictly, others leniently.

You'll also run across another group. We're the ones who don't accept late papers at all. I say "we" because I'm including myself. On the first day of every course, I announce that late papers will not be accepted "except under extraordinary circumstances." "Late" for me means one minute after the end of the class period on the day the paper is due. "Extraordinary circumstances" are those in which students are physically or emotionally incapacitated, e.g., personal crisis or severe illness.

By the way, I never request notes of confirmation from the dean's office or the infirmary. If someone claims to be the victim of extraordinary circumstances, I always believe the assertion. Over the years, certain students may have fooled me, but I suspect that most who raise the possibility of their deserving an extension ultimately confess something like "I guess I'm not that sick." Then they pay the penalty, and we both move on.

Nonetheless, every couple of years one or two members of my classes end up peeved. They believe that because they have extra work or an outside project, they warrant special dispensation. I've discovered, though, that every student has some burden, whether a varsity sport, a theatrical production, a job, or a particularly rigorous program. Thus the student who knows about an assigned paper four or five weeks before it's expected, but still waits until the last minute to start, doesn't receive great sympathy from me.

I may sound harsh. Most of my students, however, approve the policy because it guarantees that everyone is treated equally, a principle both teachers and students esteem. This rule also helps me avoid deciding whether a paper submitted three hours late deserves the same penalty as one handed in two days late.

Finally, and particularly important, this system demands that students act like adults. One of the rules of most jobs is that when something is due, it's due. Operations can't wait because the surgeon isn't ready. Courtroom trials proceed on time. Magazines have deadlines. The adult world is a place of due dates, not postponements.

Occasionally you may suffer serious illness or severe personal stress, but no teacher wants to hear about a wild weekend that left you exhausted.

I'm back to that word again: self-discipline. When a paper is expected Monday at 10:00 a.m., don't dawdle until 9:55 to print it, because the line at the library machine may be long or the printer jammed. If you're allowed to send the paper as an e-mail attachment, don't wait until thirty seconds before the final moment. Things happen.

Some teachers will claim that you should expect to do six or eight drafts of each essay. They may even brag about one of their own endeavors, currently in its ninth version, and which they still don't have right.

I'm not telling you to anticipate that much work. No students have time to so indulge themselves, and you do have a life outside this one assignment.

But I'll repeat my suggestion once more. Start early. No paper is ever absolutely finished, for reworking is always possible. Nevertheless, you do have to submit these things. You should expect to complete a draft or two, revise thoroughly, then reprint. If you have time for more, great. If you're rushed, do the best you can.

I've mocked myself enough in this book that I hope you don't mind some self-congratulation. One of my stronger qualities as a student was my capacity to complete papers promptly. I'm not claiming that all were masterpieces, but I did usually finish with time to spare. I'm sure that this ability helped me, so perhaps that's one reason I'm tough on my own students.

In sum, even if your teacher is easygoing about deadlines, make yourself stick by them. In the long run, maintaining such a strategy will work for you, not to mention provide peace of mind.

~⸙~

Toward the latter part of every semester, usually when I distribute the final paper assignment, I remind all my classes that during the upcoming weeks they will be inundated with projects and examinations. Moreover, through no fault of their own, they probably have too little time to complete comfortably all the work that lies ahead. Yet the most telling measure of how much they have benefited from college is how they survive under this pressure.

If they find themselves staying up three or four nights in a row and driving themselves into collapse, then they have failed. However their grades turn out, in the most important sense they have failed.

If, on the other hand, they plan their time, prepare and submit all work promptly with as effective an effort as they can reasonably expect from themselves, and if they otherwise remain in control, then they have demonstrated the maturity and self-discipline that will serve them well, no matter where their lives lead.

Chapter Eight

Working With the Faculty

VISITING

To this point we've talked about the faculty primarily from a distance. They're in front of the classroom; you're in your seat watching, listening, and responding. But professors are also human beings with personal sides, and by not taking advantage you're missing out on an important part of the college experience.

Thus my first suggestion: try to visit all of your instructors in their offices at least once a semester. That's the only way you're going to know them.

A lot of you probably think I mean that you should visit when you have a problem. Not at all. Even if everything's going smoothly, stop by to talk. Virtually all teachers have regular office hours, ranging from one a week to as many as ten. In addition, you can meet almost anybody if you arrange an appointment.

You'll discover that some instructors who seem forbidding in class are more relaxed in private, where they deal with students one on one. You can use the course material as a starting point, but don't be afraid to widen the discussion to cover the rest of your college career: the major, course selections, options for graduate or professional school, even jobs. Many of us are also pleased to share our own experiences in these areas.

If you do have a problem, don't be afraid to bring that up. Teachers want to assist. Talking to you is, for some of us, the most enjoyable part of our jobs. Yet we can't help if you don't ask.

Realize, though, that some professors will not be eager to see you. They may begrudge you a moment or two, but then they'll send you away. They don't want to discuss your papers, grades, or exams, and they don't want to hear your career plans. They certainly won't be interested in idle chatter. They're willing to work with you in a classroom, and correct what you write, but that's all. If you run into such instructors, don't take their attitude personally. A few chapters ago, we considered other tasks professors must discharge. Assume the ones who dismiss you are so encumbered, and head off.

In the end, you don't need twenty teachers on your team. If you know two or three well, you're doing fine.

Don't fall into the familiar student malaise and grumble that nobody cares about you. A lot of us do. Yet in a given semester, a professor may have anywhere from a hundred to a thousand students and advisees, while you have only four or five teachers. With those odds, you have to make the extra effort.

One important rule about visiting teachers: when you schedule an appointment, be sure to arrive—and on time. Few things annoy a professor more than appearing at school specifically for a student conference, then waiting for that student, who never shows. Or who does show, but a half-hour late. Even if you arrange a time during regular office hours, when the professor is supposed to be there anyway, you're still expected. Therefore if you cannot make the meeting, have the courtesy to call or e-mail. If you're going to be late, the same rule applies.

Sometimes the reverse will occur: you'll be on time, but the teacher won't. In that case, remain patient. Instructors may be detained by classes or meetings that run long, so wait at least ten minutes before taking action. Even then, don't assail the department secretary for an explanation. Inquire politely. If the teacher never arrives, leave a note with your phone number or e-mail address. Not all professors will respond, but at least you will have observed the amenities.

CONCERNING PAPERS

When you do find a receptive professor, don't hesitate to solicit help. For instance, suppose you're struggling with an essay. Ask about the viability of your topic. The teacher may narrow your focus or outline how the paper could proceed. Some instructors will go so far as to review an early draft, pointing out where it could be strengthened.

Don't expect all teachers to react this way. But if some are willing to help, don't dismiss their contributions.

Let's assume that in the process of writing, you've appropriated ideas from another source. Such borrowing falls into two categories: (1) direct quotations and (2) general concepts. Most students are aware that they must acknowledge direct quotations. Some are unaware that they must acknowledge concepts.

Don't carry this precept to an extreme. To write "Abraham Lincoln was the sixteenth president of the United States" and footnote such information is ludicrous. When a fact or thought has been stated so often that it is part of the general consciousness, or in "public domain," don't footnote it. When, on the other hand, you're rewriting someone else's original opinion, acknowledge it. If in doubt, better to over-footnote than under-footnote.

On a rare occasion you might, either through laziness or a less noble instinct, consider quoting without identifying the source. You might even be desperate enough to steal an entire essay from a local or an on-line provider.

Don't. And not just because of ethical reasons. The price of being caught is too high.

Stealing someone else's ideas, and that's what we're talking about, is known as "plagiarism," and it is one of the worst missteps you can take at college. If the transgression is discovered, the teacher will be forced to drag you and your work before an academic integrity board, you will probably fail the course, and you will likely be suspended or expelled.

Never assume that your teacher will not recognize the source. Assume instead that it is lying open on a desk at home. Even if you appropriate material from an obscure website that you are convinced no one else has ever found, you're asking for trouble.

One more word about plagiarism. If you do steal a paper, and your crime remains undetected, you'll feel rotten. Even if you escape with a great grade, you'll still feel rotten.

Let me finish this unpleasant interlude by turning once more to the honorable among you. If you want to include supplementary material, but are uncertain whether to cite it, check with your instructor.

Let's also agree that when presenting citations, you do not create your own style of documentation. Few qualities make a paper appear amateurish more than an idiosyncratic footnote form. Some teachers will hand such work right back to you, with the strong request that you redo it properly.

Proper form is no harder to apply than your own formula. Therefore use one of the numerous guides, like *The MLA Handbook*, and follow the models therein. The time spent is minimal and the rewards substantial. Proper footnotes and bibliography are the signs of a serious student. Otherwise you look fatuous, no matter what your content.

Remember to make a copy of your work, or at least to keep it on a backup disk or the hard drive of your computer. Should the unthinkable occur, and the instructor lose your essay, as happens, you don't want to rewrite from zero.

Proofread your papers. This procedure may be distressing, for it involves reading what you've written, but don't submit an essay that's full of typographical errors. Take time to read and correct. Besides, given the number of correcting mechanisms on computers, a lot of this toil will be done for you automatically.

No teacher expects flawless work. At least, most don't. We do, however, hope that you'll have sufficient pride to care about what you submit. Nothing you do in college more accurately represents the quality of your mind than your writing. Ask yourself what you would think of the person who offered yours. If it's a mess, take suitable action.

Let's say that after completing all these steps, you realize that your paper is not as good as you had hoped. You've rushed, and you know that the piece is shoddy. But deadlines are deadlines, so you submit it with an apology: "I know it's not much, but I'll do better next time." Maybe you attach a prefatory note to the paper itself.

Why would you make such a gesture? You calculate that if you display such candor, the teacher might be impressed and grade generously.

You're wrong. Teachers, as I regularly remind you, are human, and they'll follow your suggestion. If you inform them that the paper is a disappointment, they'll read it with that evaluation in mind, and they'll tend to give you a lower mark under the assumption that you'll have no reason to complain.

Besides, if you don't say anything, the teacher may find some quality in the work that you missed, and you could end up with a higher grade than you expected.

COMPLAINTS

The last contingency happens all too rarely. Far more often, you present what you think is a first-class job, but after one week or six, depending on the professor's pace, the paper is returned with a discouraging result. Do you simply shrug and sulk?

You know what I'm going to propose. Take that paper and proceed directly to the professor's office. Don't walk in looking for a fight. That attitude is bound to engender resistance. What you are seeking, you indicate politely, is help. How might you have made this paper better? And what can you do to improve on the next one?

This approach is valuable even if the grade is satisfactory. Perhaps the teacher has attached very few comments, or perhaps those scribbles are confusing. Request an explanation.

You're not playing up. You're trying to learn.

Even on these occasions, certain teachers will tell you that they are busy, or that they don't care to discuss the matter. At a university, with its massive course enrollments, you may discover that the professor has never read your paper, that it was corrected by a graduate assistant in whose direction you will be ushered. At a small college, the professor may tell you to find someone who specializes in the teaching of writing. In any case, if a teacher refuses to review a paper, you have to accept the decision.

Few of us, however, will be so aloof. Most will agree to a conference, and for you such a session can offer several rewards.

Teachers who want to be helpful will probably examine the paper more closely than you expected. Some who are especially diligent will even reread your work word by word, offering constructive commentary along the way. We speak faster than we write, and when correcting a mass of papers we have neither time nor patience to record every subtle reaction. In speaking privately, however, we can articulate our ideas with greater specificity.

Be prepared, by the way, for different standards from different professors. An overall approach to a subject might earn an A from one and a B- from another. A writing style that appeals to one teacher might offend another. A theory that impresses one teacher might seem so much balderdash to another. When you come across conflicting attitudes, don't play instructors against each other. You'll lose. Decide for yourself whose judgment you accept.

This lesson has a positive side. Every teacher offers something special. From one you will learn about research techniques, from another writing style, from another an intriguing critical perspective. We all have individual concerns. Put them together, and what you have is part of your education.

After reviewing papers with five or ten teachers, you're going to be a more perceptive and adept writer. That achievement will also help you fulfill your overall college goal: to prepare for life.

On rare occasions, a teacher will reread a paper and decide that the grade was unfair, that you deserved a higher mark. Don't anticipate this outcome, but don't reject it, either.

I don't think a teacher would actually lower a grade in the office, but on occasion I've told a student that on second reading I've realized I was too generous. At such moments, we both learn, as standards become clarified, and the student is aware that next time grading will be tougher.

Very occasionally a teacher will let you rewrite a paper. In composition courses this opportunity is more common, but elsewhere, too, it might be permitted. If you do rewrite, the reward may be not a new grade but only the chance to improve your skills. Should a new grade be involved, fine. If not, take advantage of the teacher's willingness to read your additional effort. You can only become a more effective writer.

PROBLEMS WITH TEACHERS

I would be negligent if I did not acknowledge that certain professors can be difficult. I'm not speaking of those who are boring lecturers or hard graders. Some professors, like people in every branch of society, are unreasonable, unfair, and unsympathetic. You're going to meet folks who simply irritate you, or who strike you as unforgivably narrow-minded and egotistical. Or worse.

For example, be on guard for those professors who try to impose their own intellectual or political leanings. I don't mean instructors who openly acknowledge their personal perspectives. We all have such viewpoints, but many of us also invite disagreement, and the resulting give-and-take can be enriching and enjoyable. No, I'm speaking of those teachers who operate under the conviction that their opinions are the only correct ones, and woe betide anyone who has the gumption to disagree. On papers and examinations, any divergence from the professor's established line ensures a low or even failing grade, while during class meetings discordant voices are dismissed high-handedly. You may protest, perhaps during class, perhaps in the privacy of an office, but the chances are that any professors who crush dissent will not be intimidated by confrontation, public or not. Indeed, they may relish it. And they probably have tenure, too.

I could dramatize more unpleasant situations, but my point would be the same: if you discover early in a course that your professor truly antagonizes you, drop it. Life is too short and college too potentially valuable for you to endure unnecessary agony. If you discover the reality so late that withdrawing is not practical, you won't suffer alone. Others will be available for commiseration, so do the best you can. I suppose that even these experiences are of some worth, for they toughen you up for the outside world, where annoying people pop up every day.

I must mention, however, one particular variety of unpleasantness against which you should take action. This section is written primarily, but not solely, for female students.

Sexual harassment remains a fact of life, and the college campus, though in some ways a haven, is nonetheless part of life. Here, too, people take advantage of one another.

Professors who indulge in sexual games or power displays are less common than they once were, but they still lurk. They often begin by inviting students to lunch or dinner. The invitations may seem harmless, but they can be the prelude to relentless pursuit, during which these miscreants conduct awfully clever campaigns. When challenged about their intentions, they retreat behind a facade of innocence: "I only asked her to have coffee downtown."

Not every teacher who invites you for lunch or a drink is a threat, but be circumspect. If one seems excessively curious about your private life or dating habits, or if you feel in any way uneasy, leave the premises. And if a high grade or some other bonus is promised in exchange for sexual favors, turn at once to the school committee on sexual harassment or another campus official. Not only are you protecting yourself; you may be helping others who have been or could be victimized.

Males, too, are vulnerable. A friend of mine told me a story from his college days, when he wondered why no matter how strong his papers in one course, they received no better than C. He was later informed that the teacher, male, gave higher grades only to those students, male, who slept with him. It happens, readers.

Given the close nature of a college environment, sexual harassment is an omnipresent threat. If it appears, I reiterate advice given earlier in a different context: talk to somebody.

LETTERS OF RECOMMENDATION

I don't want to end this chapter on a depressing note, so I'll switch to a more optimistic subject. Let's say that as a freshman you do superbly in one course. You've also talked at length with the teacher, and you recognize that here is someone from whom you may one day want a letter of recommendation for either graduate school or a job.

Now is the time to ask for that letter and to have it placed in a permanent dossier at school. Virtually every institution has an office for career placement where notices of jobs are advertised, counselors help you prepare a résumé, and you can maintain a credential file that include letters of recommendation. Most students wait until their senior years to open such a file, but smart students begin theirs as soon as they work with a professor from whom they would like a reference.

Why put in the letter right away? The professor you know as a freshman may not be around when you're a senior. Teachers take sabbaticals, change schools, or retire. Furthermore, when you're currently on a teacher's mind, the letter can be filled with detail, and the more specific the recommendation, the greater its impact. Thus when you have teachers who know and like you, ask them to write immediately at semester's end, and provide them with a form for the placement service. In case you take another course with those teachers, a likely occurrence since they've admired your work and helped you, original letters can be updated. But in the event any of these folks leave your life, you have a record of accomplishment.

Letters of recommendation are usually written on or attached to official school forms, and on these you will be asked whether you waive the right to see them. The law gives you this privilege. If you waive it, professors know that they are writing a confidential document.

The decision is yours. Recognize, however, that professors feel more secure when they know that you will not check their work, and readers of such letters often take them more seriously. Don't worry that your professors will write something damaging. If they believe they cannot be sufficiently positive, they'll tell you to find someone else.

Let me end this chapter with a final word of encouragement. We college teachers revel in our individuality, far more than members of most other professions. Don't expect us to be all alike. Indeed, be glad we're not, for our uniqueness is part of our appeal. As a whole, however, we do have one characteristic in common: we enjoy our subject, and our good fortune is to spend our lives studying and sharing it with others, particularly you. For us to succeed, you must be willing to work with us. Give us the chance to help.

Chapter Nine

Beyond the Classroom

The focus of this book, as if you were not aware, has been your academic development at college, specifically your choice of courses and teachers, and the most effective ways to learn from both. A college education, though, has many aspects, and I'll comment on a few.

LIVING AT COLLEGE

I have no way to determine how much the college environment itself will shape you, for I have no idea whom or what you will encounter. All I know is that you are bound to meet extremes of every sort, and you must be prepared to take a stand on how to behave. In doing so, you may learn more than any class can teach. On the other hand, if you handle this part of life foolishly, all the other strategies we've discussed will be wasted. So I'll offer a few reflections, beginning with the decidedly less weighty.

Provisions

What should you bring from home?

I'll leave the matter of apparel to you. At most schools, a few students are slave to the whims of fashion, and fret about designer clothes and other trends, but don't let such frivolities dominate your existence, because no one who ought to matter pays attention to them. For the rest of you, choice of wardrobe should rest on geography as much as taste. My only recommendation is to bring one outfit appropriate for a formal occasion. Otherwise do as faculty members do: present yourself however you want.

I should add that you're currently reading the words of someone who wears a suit and tie to every class. Then again, I'm virtually the only professor on my campus who maintains that practice.

With regard to room supplies, remember that you'll be living at college for two-thirds of the year; in fact, some of you will so enjoy the environs that you'll spend summers as well. Thus if you have accoutrements from home that will make life more pleasant, bring them.

Some of them, that is. Remember, too, that you'll acquire paraphernalia of all kinds, and your room will clutter up. Therefore limit what you tote from home. When in doubt, leave things behind.

If you can, visit your school before arriving in the fall to give yourself an idea what kind of room and furnishings you should expect. If such a trip is unfeasible, call the housing office to find out whether sheets, towels, and blankets are provided. You may be sent a list of such information. In any case, bring a few extra linens as well as several hangers. Bring an umbrella. Ask whether you'll need pillows or a desk lamp.

During the summer before your freshman year, the college will give you the name, address, and phone number of your assigned roommate, so that by the time the two of you arrive, you'll be acquainted. During these preliminary conversations, you can also decide who will bring a refrigerator or other amenities.

Whatever you have between you, don't overdo these supplies.

To bolster your academic side, if you have a personal work implement, like a favorite binder or writing board, pack it. Otherwise assume that the school store will stock all the stationery equipment you'll ever use.

Bring or buy a dictionary and a thesaurus (a synonym book). Both are invaluable reference tools.

Most important, if you have a personal computer, bring it (as I hardly need remind you). The school itself will probably supply hundreds of machines, but having your own is highly desirable. Some colleges give every student a computer. If so, great. If not, take whatever action you can to outfit yourself properly.

If you have a book to which you are devoted, like a novel you often reread, you'll be pleased to have it with you. But don't haul up a couple of cartons' worth. The library nearby will contain any volume you want.

If music is an important part of your life, and your computer or iPod does not satisfy this need, you might bring a CD player with a limited number of discs. Don't, however, drag up your entire collection. So many people will have players, and so many discs will be floating around the dorm, that you'll have access to a limitless supply. Bring a few, replaceable favorites. You can borrow the rest.

Note that word in the last paragraph: "replaceable." Keep in mind that you'll be living in a college dormitory, where no one's possessions are sacred, and vandalism is rampant. People will burst into your room at any time. If you're there, you won't easily turn down a friend who requests a CD that means a lot to you. If you're not there, expect some intruders to help themselves to your discs and anything else of interest. The technical term is "stealing."

What's the lesson? Try not to bring to college anything that you cannot afford to leave at college. Even a good friend with only the best of intentions may fall on your expensive new DVD player. If you're not prepared to see something ruined, and you can do without it, don't bring it.

The same for room decorations. A couple of pictures or posters are invaluable in giving you a sense of home, that your room is where you live, not just exist. Do not, however, bring a family heirloom with historical value. I guarantee that the first time anyone spills an ice cream sundae in your room, the hot fudge will land right on an irreplaceable photograph.

The same with furniture. If you want a piece that makes you feel cozy, be sure it's solid enough to take the pounding of a hundred thoughtless visitors.

One accessory to leave at home is a television. Until recently, hardly anyone brought a set to college, but now the mood of the campus has changed, and so have televisions. If you own a portable one, you may be tempted to pile it in just to keep up with the latest soap or nighttime series, or whatever keeps you occupied at home.

Forget it. You know how much time television wastes. Maybe you don't, but trust me: hours can fly by. And never fool yourself that you'll limit your watching to a few select shows. By the time you turn on the set early "to warm it up," stick around afterwards for one more show, then turn it back on to pass a casual hour before going to sleep, you'll be throwing away huge blocks of time. Even with digital video recorders and TiVo, you'll arrange your schedule to watch particular shows.

Television's a drug, and withdrawal is tough. But if you become involved in college life, you'll forget about television. Besides, if you're desperate to see a particular show, someone down the hall is bound to have a set.

Remember, too, that with a computer, you'll be distracted by video games, chat rooms, and all its other countless inducements. You don't need television.

You may be astonished to learn that when I went to school, no one brought a television. Indeed, only a few folks had radios or "record players," as they were then called. Such deprivation had benefits, though, for we had many fewer distractions. One result of all the amusements that life currently offers is that you have to battle much harder to focus on your priorities.

If you're fortunate enough to own a car, you'll probably drive it up, for it inspires an exultant feeling of freedom. Be aware, though, that your colleagues without a vehicle will expect you to render regular transportation, sometimes when you have no inclination to do so. In that case, they will ask to borrow your car, perhaps for a trip downtown, perhaps for a five-hundred-mile trek. I have no idea about the insurance risks, but prepare to worry about such issues, as well as campus registration rules and limited parking. Don't let me discourage you from bringing the car (as if I could). It can be a great help, particularly if your school is isolated. But be ready for problems.

Health

When you live alone for the first time, you can become so involved in your daily life that you forget the most basic aspects of taking care of yourself. I'll mention a few.

Everyone around you will probably live amid a litter of clothes, shoes, papers, books, and dust. College apartments are notorious messes, in which a leftover pizza carton passes for contemporary American décor. You may choose to live this way, too. Nothing tragic here. Just accept a single bit of advice. Once a month, clean the room. You can never tell what or whom you'll find underneath that pile of dirty laundry.

Wash that laundry, too, or one day you'll discover that your laundry bag and your dresser have switched roles.

On a more serious note, be careful about what you eat. Pizza, donuts, and nacho chips do not constitute the three basic food groups. Try to achieve a balanced diet, and arrange your schedule so you eat at regular times. Cafeteria food may not satisfy all your needs. (Pardon me. Cafeteria food *will* not satisfy all your needs.) Nevertheless, do what you can to maintain a healthful diet. With all the information about food circulating through the media, you don't need my help in determining what's salubrious. All I'll say is that if you don't eat right, you won't feel right. And if you don't feel right, you can't work right. Make sure you leave time for proper breakfasts, lunches, and suppers. Then go.

No doubt your college will offer a food plan, according to which you pay in advance to eat in a school dining hall. Eventually you may wish to turn down such an arrangement, but for the first semester or year I'd accept it. Opening weeks are confusing enough without the added worry of where to find every meal. When you become familiar with the community and the preferable restaurants, or when you move off-campus and cook for yourself, leave the cafeterias. Until that time, let the school handle one task in your life.

My last word on health is about sleep. Nothing seems to make college students prouder than to announce that they've stayed up until four in the morning. Not to work, you understand. Just to stay up. Yet you know that one way to leave yourself a physical and psychological wreck is to neglect sleep.

At the beginning of your undergraduate career, when you're still giddy over the realization that no one's keeping track of you, your favorite method of demonstrating emancipation will be to stay up late and do who-knows-what. I won't bother telling you to skip this stage because I know that even the brightest among you must experience it. After you've gone sleepless for a few nights, though, and made yourself good and sick, learn the lesson. You need sleep. The more regular your hours and habits, the more organized your life.

I know that on certain nights you'll be desperate to let loose, and one way to do so is to stay up until all hours. Just don't make a fool of yourself by staying up every night, or you'll end up in the infirmary. Where they tell you precisely when to go to sleep.

Roommates

The very word strikes terror. Roommates can be a source of such misery as to cast a pall over your whole life. They can also turn into lasting friends. In either case, your roommate will be the first person you know, and thus this individual is worth a moment's thought.

At the outset of your college experience, when you may end up meandering by yourself, be grateful for a roommate, who will probably ease the pressures of visiting other new dorm occupants or sitting at a dining-room table with strangers. In addition, walking into an extracurricular or social activity is less unnerving when two of you enter together. A roommate is also likely to bring a new circle of acquaintances into your life. Most important, a roommate is someone with whom you can talk or work out a problem. True, the roommate may create different problems, but even if you sense initial irritations, give this person a chance. Before long the term will be over; then you can go elsewhere.

Of course, if your roommate's habits are completely obnoxious, all bets are off. I'm not talking about someone who's merely sloppy or dresses funny, plays the wrong music, makes stupid jokes, and uses what you judge to be inappropriate language. I'm talking about serious conflicts.

For instance, at a lot of colleges, smoking inside school buildings is banned, but you might still prefer someone who has a total aversion to tobacco. Thus you request a nonsmoker for a roommate. If, however, five minutes into your first meeting, this person lights up, complain to the housing authority. They may not take immediate action, but plenty of other people will want to move out of their own rooms for numerous reasons, so regularly remind the office of your dilemma.

I know one young woman who was actually allergic to cigarette smoke, and indicated as much on her dormitory selection form. Yet when over the summer she spoke to her assigned roommate, the other girl raved about the joys of smoking. The first girl's father then called the college housing office to explain that his daughter had nowhere to stay. An assistant claimed that the student did, and, besides, no other rooms were available. The father then retorted that his daughter couldn't live in a space that made her violently ill, and demanded to speak with the director of housing. After two more calls, which included the father's threat to take the matter up the administrative ladder and speak with one dean after another, the housing office managed to find alternate accommodations.

Let's also hypothesize a more extreme contingency. Suppose you come across a roommate involved in what you determine to be dangerous or illegal behavior, e.g., firearms or drugs. Under those circumstances, complain extremely firmly. I am not telling you to be a police informant. I am suggesting only that you protect yourself. If the housing authorities are indecisive, take your complaint to that infamous ladder until you find someone who takes action. Make clear to everyone with whom you speak that you expect the college to do all it can to protect your right to live and work in safety.

Let's not dwell, however, on the ugly side of the roommate question. Let's imagine instead that this new associate will be a congenial figure who brings a different background and set of values to your college experience, and who teaches you to look at school and life from a new perspective. If that end can be achieved with a minimum of fuss, you are fortunate, indeed.

Social Life

Your roommate may be the person on campus you know most intimately, but plenty of others will be available, particularly in the building where you live. This subject brings us back to the beginning of the book, where I mentioned the dormitory preference form that accompanied your letter of acceptance. One question that should catch your attention is whether you prefer a single-sex or coed dorm space. Some institutions even allow upper-level males and females to share the same room, an arrangement that may be one reason you're eager to go to college.

I'd feel awkward telling you which setup to choose, because I'm not sure. When I went to school, all dorms were single-sex. My students tell me that coed dorms work out wonderfully, and they add something about brother-sister relationships. Fair enough. I also have the impression that coed dorms, which are becoming more and more the custom, attract a friskier populace, although every school and every dorm is different.

Choose the kind of place you want. If you discover you've misjudged, you'll have opportunity to change.

Given the existence of Facebook and countless other mechanisms, online and off, that promote social interaction, the dormitory scene can be chaotic. Enjoy it, but don't let it control you. Not all colleges are as wild as the stories that students tell and that contemporary movies dramatize, but some definitely are. Whatever the truth, you'll tend to believe adventures that others relate, and you may be convinced that everyone else is sharing endless debaucheries, sexual and otherwise, that are worthy of a Roman emperor.

No matter what you hear and see, don't feel compelled to live a life racier than is comfortable for you. If you are used to the fast lane, don't slow down on my account. But if you're accustomed to a more conservative speed, you'll find others content to travel at your pace.

To women, I add an additional warning. It concerns sexual harassment, which appears generally in two forms.

The first includes demeaning remarks or gestures. These may be subtle or overt, and they're certainly annoying, but I'm not convinced that they warrant legal action, although opinions on the matter differ.

What always deserves serious response is the other form of assault known as "date rape." An attack may occur during a private moment between two people or at a party where mass intoxication negates all decency. Under any conditions, if you believe that you have been violated, report what has happened. When possible, bring a corroborating witness. Every campus has a rape or crisis center where understanding counselors wait to help. Let them.

Fraternities and Sororities

You may, for many reasons, seek this alternative to dormitory life. Again, however, I invoke the phrase "be careful."

There is no limit to the nonsense of which college students are capable. In fact, this capacity is part of their charm. Yet such fun can be destructive, and here's where the Greek houses come to the fore. Too often they legitimize behavior that outside the campus would be classified as felonious.

I know that certain houses raise money in constructive ways, then donate the profits to worthy causes, while others groups create environments that promote profound friendships Yet ask members of most houses what remains their salient college memory, and I guarantee that it will be some version of "the night we all got smashed and set fire to the post office."

Pass by a college's fraternity row the day after school lets out for the summer. Most of the buildings have to be fumigated to rid them of the putrid air.

By definition fraternities and sororities are discriminatory. I exclude, of course, those that welcome anyone who applies, and for whom a room is available. In the rest, though, members end up living with people just like themselves, reinforcing prejudices.

We also need not go into particulars of pledging and initiations. Though in most places hazing has been outlawed, tortures and humiliations are still inflicted under the guise of "fun," and every year students are crippled or even killed at the hands of sadistic "brothers" and "sisters."

You may be fortunate to find a fraternity or sorority that suits your values, but be wary of risks the wrong houses pose.

Off-Campus

The previous couple of sections may seem like a series of dire warnings about the perils of campus existence. I don't mean to sound alarmist, because a great many students enjoy that life and find it fulfilling, even educational.

Others, however, find the rowdiness intolerable, and therefore retreat off-campus, where they assume that privacy will solve all problems.

Yet beware of this recourse, too. Living alone can lead to isolation, especially if you are by nature retiring. After classes end, you may be tempted to scamper home, denying yourself participation in other college programs.

When, on the other hand, you live in the dorm, and friends announce that they're attending some useful activity, you're likely to join them. Furthermore, those endless late-night conversations about life, love, and everything else can be in their own way beneficial.

Even if you share off-campus quarters with a friend or two, don't figure that a downtown apartment is paradise, for that existence has its own hazards. Annoying, dangerous people lurk everywhere, and when you're off-campus, college security officers can't help. Cooking, cleaning, and otherwise servicing your home are time-consuming, and when something breaks, you're on your own about repairs.

Thus when you ponder the big move, ask yourself whether a change in roommate or dorm would make a difference. If the answer is "yes," mull over trying a new location at school. If the answer is "no," that the very nature of dormitory life repels you, then consider the off-campus world.

Drugs and Alcohol

Several recent books about college, written by people far closer to your age than I, treat this subject as just another sidelight, like parking problems or the availability of squash courts. I can't be that casual.

I'm not naive. Well, maybe I am, but I'm not blind to reality. Quite a few of you reading this book have used drugs. Perhaps you are regular users. A vast portion of you have imbibed alcohol, and some are probably steady drinkers. No doubt a few of you are alcoholics, even if you are unaware of the fact.

Whatever you've done in this direction, you've probably had to operate surreptitiously. In high school, whether you live at home or at boarding school, obtaining these materials is a hurdle because you're young. At least I think so. Perhaps experience has taught you that you can find whatever you want whenever you want it. I do know, however, that at college, virtually any college, illegal substances are everywhere. So are dealers and users. Right down the hall, you will meet acquaintances who indulge in every drug and drink you've ever heard of, and quite a few you've never heard of. Almost every day you will be asked to partake of something you know you shouldn't have.

That's why in a book devoted to matters academic, I feel compelled to write about this subject. You may triumph in the classroom, but if you surrender to certain forces around you, your achievements will be for naught.

I don't drink or smoke. I say so not out of self-righteousness, but only because such is the case. I admit, too, that I've never tried drugs of any kind, not even when I was at college during the swinging sixties. (In other words, I never smoked, and I never inhaled.) But I've seen students come to school innocent of these habits, then exit a year or two later broken and dependent. I've seen students who survive all four years, but after staggering through one binge after another, leave with their life in a shambles.

And I'm naive. Imagine what I'd have to say if I knew this world up close, as many of you do.

What scares me most is the attitude exemplified by a student I once encountered who was smoking a cigarette. Not marijuana, mind you. Just a plain cigarette. I was feeling virtuous at the time, so I said something like, "You know that's killing you. How can you do that to yourself?" He didn't become angry but replied, "Hey, I like it. And if I want to kill myself, it's my life, isn't it?"

I didn't know what to say.

I also don't want to preach, so I'll conclude quickly.

About alcohol. If you take a legal drink at dinner, okay. If you can drink legally, and one night you celebrate too zestily and finish by throwing up, that's forgivable. If a few nights each year you drink so much that you end up making a fool of yourself, I won't be proud of you, but I comprehend that sometimes you have to let off steam.

But if you drink to such an extent that any really good time requires the abuse of alcohol, then you have my sympathy, for I suspect you'll soon be unable to have any fun without it.

About drugs. At college you can become lonely, frustrated, and angry. Work can pile up. You can lose sleep. You can have a terrible fight with a friend. You can fail a series of tests or papers. You can be besieged by problems until you feel hopelessly depressed. And on every side friends will offer escape through drugs.

Listen to music instead. Watch television. Go to a movie. Run around the gym. Talk to teachers, administrators, or reliable friends. Visit the medical and emotional counseling services.

If all this doesn't help, go home for a few days. If that option isn't practical, take a brief vacation from school. Do anything to clear your mind. No college obligation is so vital that you should endanger your well-being.

Don't turn to drugs.

~~~

In rereading the last sections, I realize that my tone has turned slightly morbid. I apologize, because my intention is not to leave you in a permanent funk.

A college campus can be a wonderful place, where many opportunities await, and you have the chance to grow immeasurably. Moreover, I hope you leave for college with the firm expectation that these four years will be a happy and pivotal part of your life.

Yet risks abound, and you have to maintain your standards.

College freedom allows you to enjoy adult pleasures. These also demand that you assume adult responsibilities.

Have a fine time.

EXTRACURRICULAR LIFE

Speaking of a fine time, we've noted how certain aspects of a college education may be tightly structured, but that many more are likely to be freewheeling. As I suggested in our first chapter, part of your learning experience will be the people you encounter, and you should try to meet them in many settings. I'll pose a few.

I met some of my best friends in physical education classes, where people tend to shed pretensions. You'd be amazed what a good time can be had in handball.

Here is the place to add that at college you can be as adventurous athletically as you can academically. Most schools offer classes in many sports, from the beginning level on up. Have you ever wanted to try racquetball, volleyball, table tennis, golf, fencing, dance, aerobics, or any of a dozen others? Your institution probably offers team intramural competitions in softball, basketball, and even frisbee. You may not be varsity material, but don't become sedentary in the name of learning. You're entitled to fun and, besides, vigorous activity is healthful. You'll also learn something about the sport, the nature of competition, and yourself.

If you don't want to join a class or compete, maybe you'd prefer to jog or lift weights according to your own routine. If that kind of program is too demanding, at least take a walk. Most campuses are attractive places. Stroll. Take in the sights.

Do something.

Now to extracurriculars. In high school you probably joined these activities with the thought of having some to enumerate on college applications. Indeed, the word "extracurriculars" probably retains a childish quality, as though their primary use was to impress admissions officers.

At college, you join activities only because you enjoy them. You also seek skills and experience that will help you prepare for life after school.

The college newspaper is always a sprightly place, and contributing there will keep you abreast of campus issues and personalities. If you move into a leadership position, you'll find yourself a figure of authority and controversy, status that might be appealing. If you're interested in other aspects of the media, try the radio, the television station, or the yearbook.

Every school has political societies, where students ranging from the most conservative to the most liberal join like-minded thinkers. Passions here run hot, so if you become affiliated with such a group, be prepared for rousing times. These organizations also undertake all sorts of potentially contentious activity: speaking and acting against what they judge to be campus inequities, inviting controversial guests, and joining the electoral process on the municipal, state, and national levels. For those who anticipate a career in the public arena, a college campus can provide superb training ground.

If you're a budding writer, try the literary magazine, where you'll encounter other talented and ambitious souls. You'll also meet editors who will be honest about their tastes, so you may endure the pain of rejection, but you will likely also savor the exaltation of seeing your efforts in print. Finally, you might make connections that will aid your efforts to publish beyond the campus.

Dozens of other organizations are open: musical, academic, scientific, service, social, anything you want. When you join, you're certain to meet kindred spirits, because everyone involved shares at least one concern: the work of the group.

Here I'll consider the multitudinous aspects of one such area that I happen to know well: the theater.

Suppose you've never acted before, but some voice within urges you to audition for the annual college musical. What do you have to lose? You may hate it. All right. Now you know to tell that voice to keep quiet. Or you may love the experience. From then on, you'll want that voice to ring out regularly. Either way, you can be sure that the

"Hey-kids-let's-put-on-a-show" spirit is contagious, and no one goes through a production sitting alone in a corner learning nothing.

If you don't want to put yourself out front, join the crew. Every theater department needs technical help, from set builders to stagehands. You'll avoid most of the pressure, but you'll enjoy the discipline of rehearsal, the exhilaration of performance, and the joy of camaraderie.

And the theater is just one place available to you.

Perhaps you're interested in working in a science lab, helping on a research project. Faculty always need assistants, and no experience will teach you more about the challenges and rewards of such efforts than actual participation.

Maybe you'd like to take part in a community or religious organization, working with the elderly or the young. Maybe you'd like to participate at the school counseling center or in the college government. If you can't find something, you're not looking.

Don't, however, smother yourself. The word, after all, is "extracurricular." Just keep in mind that an activity you start for fun could determine the direction of your life. How many journalists began by writing on college newspapers? Like part-time jobs or internships, extracurricular options can bring to light undiscovered abilities.

One more advantage of such projects. By taking part, you'll be aware of what's happening on campus. Every college is visited by a stream of speakers and performers. I don't expect you to race around, feverishly taking in every event that merits a poster. But when a guest of interest arrives, try to attend. Think of these events as a supplement to your classroom education. Think of them also as something different to do before you head back to the dormitory party.

ALTERNATIVE CREDIT

Let me begin to conclude this chapter by returning to the academic side and jumping ahead a couple of years.

In the latter stages of your college career, you can earn academic credit for work outside the traditional class format. All the following options are available after graduation as well as before, so pursuing them is not in accord with our familiar directive about four years devoted to the unique offerings on a campus. Since, however, these programs represent wonderful and popular opportunities, I'll toss in my two cents about each.

Studying Abroad

Many students choose to spend either a semester or a year away from their home college, studying in other countries. How enjoyable are such times? Let me put it this way: I have yet to meet a student who went abroad and did not return delighted with the experience. For students of foreign languages and literature, the program has obvious benefits. But no matter what your major field, the adventure offers such potential that I strongly recommend it.

Do not, however, go under the assumption that the academic routine there will help you very much. My impression is that, to the contrary, courses in other countries are frequently so haphazard as to become almost ancillary to the rest of the trip. To compile credits for graduation, you might have to take classes that correspond to some back home. But whatever the specific program with which you become affiliated, don't count on the class sessions for substantial intellectual stimulation. If one or two prove productive, you're lucky. Otherwise expect that the education you receive will be of a much more personal nature: meeting people, traveling within a country and in neighboring locales, and experiencing a different culture. You could master another language, and you will almost certainly acquire a breadth of understanding that will help you prepare for life. Just don't plan on classroom enrichment.

Work-Study Programs

The second option for outside credit involves what are called "field experiences" or "internships." These are jobs that demand several hours of work per week, and usually earn the equivalent of one or two courses' credit.

Such positions offer rewards, but may include a couple of problems. We've established more than once that only a certain number of courses can be taken in college, and an internship means losing a few. I know that after some classes you'll be grateful for the forfeiture. Still, you'll have jobs for the rest of your life. These four years . . . (finish this thought).

Another possible problem with an internship is that the job may disappoint you. Perhaps the employer, recognizing that you are a parttimer, ignores you. You fetch coffee, sort mail, and sharpen pencils, but never immerse yourself in the business. Another possibility is that the employer cannot grasp that you are a part-timer and therefore makes unreasonable demands on your time and energy. Your work at school suffers, the job becomes irritating, and the semester drains you.

Nonetheless, we should not overlook the potential rewards of internships. Several of my advisees, for instance, have worked at local television stations, and their experiences not only proved enjoyable and instructive, but also led to full-time positions.

Furthermore, time in the workplace may open your eyes to the realities of the nine-to-five world, as well as the tone of a particular occupation. Some of my students who spent months in a news office discovered that they loved the hustle of that profession. Others came away far less enchanted.

Jobs also provide needed breaks from campus life. No matter what the pleasures of any institution, you may, by your third or fourth year, feel confined. Internships, like travel, are respites that allow you to return with renewed inspiration.

My overall view is that a job, if it works out, is worth surrendering a couple of courses. Experience that gives you skills or opens your eyes to a career is simply too special to pass up. Besides, when you do begin your quest for a full-time job, these credentials will make you a more impressive candidate.

Independent Study

Here is the third alternative to traditional classes, and about this option I have what some would deem a controversial opinion: despite its possible benefits, this path is often overrated.

Independent study demands first that you find a subject of interest, one that usually involves considerable research, and which climaxes with an extended written project. By "extended" I mean anywhere from fifty pages on up, depending on the field and subject.

The rationale behind this effort is that it represents a chance for you to probe deeply into a specific topic. The work is also intended to give you a taste of full-time scholarly life.

On the surface, the venture may sound attractive, and for some students it works out happily. But the business is rife with pitfalls that surface more frequently than those in charge admit.

First, any project that lasts a year tends to become burdensome, even if you are motivated. For confirmation, ask professors about the frustration they endured completing their doctoral dissertations. And these people were heading toward a degree that would set them up for their life's work. You're doing yours simply for pleasure and one course credit. Therefore quite a few students who begin an independent study out of casual interest become enervated.

Don't assume, either, that the isolation of independent study matches the style of a scholar's life, because scholars don't work alone. They discuss their ideas and writing with colleagues, as you do when you take a seminar and share papers with other students. During independent study, though, you cut yourself off from everyone except your sponsor, and you miss the interaction that real scholars relish.

Another frequent problem is that the independent study clashes with other courses. During most projects, you'll meet your sponsor once a week to discuss whatever reading and writing you've completed, and at the beginning of a term such a schedule will be easy to maintain. As the semester rolls on, however, and work for other courses builds, you'll begin to postpone these meetings, even while you assure both your professor and yourself that you're doing fine on your own.

Before long, you'll delay your private project indefinitely, for teacher-imposed deadlines from a class tend to supersede self-imposed ones. Thus as the final weeks of the semester draw near, with all the papers and exams that demand attention, the independent study becomes an irritant.

Let me not, however, minimize its potential rewards. If you complete the task successfully, you'll master one area of your field, you'll develop better creative and research skills, and you'll feel pride in finishing a project of substantial length. If this result pleases your department, you may earn academic honors.

For others, however, the experience becomes a millstone. The freedom of working outside the classroom is initially alluring. When the glamour wears away, though, you may be stuck.

A couple of concluding thoughts.

I've based this book on the presumption that the vast majority of my readers plan to attend college full-time, and to complete their undergraduate work in four years.

I recognize, however, that this paradigm may not apply universally.

Some of you will enroll in a two-year or community college. Others will pursue a bachelor's degree while working full-time, caring for a family, or both, and as a result your path to graduation might extend over several more years.

I concede, too, that these and other circumstances too numerous to mention will involve complications (particularly financial) that are far beyond my scope.

Nevertheless, whatever your individual situation, I like to think that the counsel I offer is of value.

Most important, I hope that all my readers are united by one common goal: to gain as much as they can from their college experience.

Chapter Ten

Final Words

Over these chapters I've offered a batch of suggestions about how to respond when matters at college go wrong. I've done so under the assumption that whatever roadblocks you encounter, you can overcome them.

What happens, though, if you can't? What happens if despite all your initial expectation and preparation, you end up miserable?

Suppose you figured that you'd be happy at a small college, but find the scope of programs and people too narrow.

Suppose you selected a large university, but feel stranded amid the massive campus and impersonal crowds.

Suppose you were confident that you'd prefer the pace of a quiet hamlet, but realize that you revel in the whirlwind of a big city.

Suppose the school's academic and extracurricular standards prove too rigorous. Or not rigorous enough.

Suppose both your roommate and the general student populace are so unbearable that you're left friendless.

What should you do?

One alternative is to transfer. You're not wedded to this school. Hundreds of others are available, and plenty of students who flounder in an uncongenial locale flourish elsewhere.

Suppose, however, that the situation is more extreme, so that your unhappiness encompasses more than dull courses, dreary professors, or disagreeable dorm residents.

Indeed, your despair is so profound that you can no longer bear the academic environment itself.

You're fed up sitting in class. You're fed up suffering through boring texts and cranking out pointless papers and exams. You're fed up being graded and criticized. In fact, you're fed up with everything and everybody associated with higher education.

At this point you may muse on the lives of people like Abraham Lincoln, Thomas Edison, and Bill Gates, all of whom did just fine without an undergraduate degree. Maybe you decide that job training is all that counts, that the best teacher is life itself, and that anything that can be learned in college is either of no practical value or available for free on the outside. Besides, you know people your age who are already working full-time. Why allow them a head start?

In short, why should you spend the enormous amount of time and money that college demands?

If such despondency strikes, make sure you seek out all the campus resources and personnel that we considered earlier. If every one of these proves ineffective, and you see no choice but to abandon the entire undergraduate enterprise, give yourself one last chance by taking a leave: a semester or full year away. Maybe you should shift to a job that sounds stimulating or one that lets you physically release your frustration. Whatever you do, try to immerse yourself in an activity as distant from college as possible.

Such an interlude may prove salutary, so that after a few months spent enduring the rigors of the workplace, you're recharged and ready to resume school life.

Yet even this strategy has risks. Once you have sampled the outside world and perhaps the pleasures of income, you may be unwilling to surrender them for the relatively innocuous status and challenging regimen of a student.

All jobs are intrinsically limiting. Indeed, any position in any business can open only a few different doors, and for someone like you, still uncertain where you belong, defining yourself so early may be a blunder.

On the other hand, the college experience, as I have regularly reminded you, offers innumerable possibilities, so if you simply terminate your academic career, you toss away the chance to encounter a person, course, or activity that could prove decisive.

Remember, too, that you never know where or when this singular influence may appear. My most important undergraduate experience was a class in expository writing. I took it not because of the teacher's reputation, or because I thought the subject sounded interesting, but because I knew that my writing wasn't what it ought to be. The teacher was underwhelmed by me. He, in turn, was not a favorite of mine, and my grade is best forgotten.

Yet the course changed my life. For the first time I realized that I enjoyed writing, and I became determined to continue. Decades later, I'm still at it.

I hope you undergo a similar epiphany.

As I draw to the end, and as you reflect on the sum of this book, you may believe that I have dwelled too much on personal gain. Where, you ask, have I emphasized the value of thinking about others, and the joy of working *for* others? You may even feel that with so many people in so many places in so much distress, the very act of going to school to achieve personal growth is selfish. You want to help *now*.

My answer is that to work for humanity most effectively, you must discover and develop as many of your talents as possible. If you limit your education, you're also limiting the ways in which you can better the world.

Thus I urge you to explore, question, try, and otherwise give yourself as many opportunities as possible. When at last you understand how to devote your energies, you will have a strong chance to do the best for yourself as well as for others.

Good luck.

About the Author

Victor L. Cahn received his A.B. from Columbia College and his M.A. and Ph.D. from New York University. He has taught at Mercersburg Academy, Pomfret School, Phillips Exeter Academy, Bowdoin College, and Skidmore College, where he is professor of English and teaches courses in Shakespeare, modern drama, and the history of drama.

He has written several books, including *Shakespeare the Playwright: A Companion to the Complete Tragedies, Histories, Comedies, and Romances* (named an Outstanding Academic Book by *Choice*); *The Plays of Shakespeare: a Thematic Guide*; *Beyond Absurdity: the Plays of Tom Stoppard*; *Gender and Power in the Plays of Harold Pinter*; and *Classroom Virtuoso: Recollections of a Life in Learning*. His articles and reviews have appeared in such diverse publications as *Modern Drama*, the *Literary Review*, the *Chronicle of Higher Education*, the *New York Times*, and *Variety*.

Dr. Cahn is the author of numerous plays, several of which have been produced off-Broadway, including the one-man show *Sherlock Solo*, which he performed. Eight of his scripts have been published in *"Roses in December" and Other Plays*. *Fit to Kill* has been published by Samuel French.